JANE'S POCKET BOOK OF MAJOR WARSHIPS

JANE'S POCKET BOOK OF MAJOR WARSHIPS

Edited by CAPTAIN JOHN E. MOORE, R.N.

COLLIER BOOKS
A Division of Macmillan Publishing Co., Inc.
New York

Macmillan Publishing Co., Inc.
866 Third Avenue, New York, N.Y. 10022
Collier Macmillan Canada, Ltd.

Library of Congress Catalog Card Number: 73-9329

First Collier Books Edition 1973
Second Printing 1976

Jane's Pocket Book of Major Warships is also published in a hardcover edition by Macmillan Publishing Co., Inc.

Printed in the United States of America

CONTENTS

Editor's Note

This book is intended as a supplement, not a rival, to JANE'S FIGHTING SHIPS which, with its far greater detail, many photographs and 15 000 ships, remains the standard reference of the navies of the world.

However, it has been felt for some time that an up-to-date portable unclassified guide to main classes only was needed for identification purposes.

For this reason drawings have been used instead of photographs, thus making clearer specific points of detail. With each drawing there are certain minimal data which should provide a fair summary of a ship's capabilities.

So that this is truly a pocket book I have selected 250 classes (representing many times that number of ships) from the thousands in the world's navies. The criteria used were the importance of the class and the likelihood of sighting it at sea. To achieve this figure a number of interesting ships has had to be left out and some classes containing only one ship omitted. To keep the size down some prolific classes with varying silhouettes have to rely on single drawings. These limitations, I am afraid, are made necessary by condensation.

The allocation of ships to various type names has become clumsy, misleading and confusing. For various reasons, budgetary, tactical or nostalgic, types are given descriptive names which bear no relation to their size, speed, armament or function. I have therefore used those guidelines to make an arbitrary division of the 250 classes into 16 main types. This may disturb some readers but simplification was necessary to achieve the aim of the book.

There are some classes (for instance, the USN 'Bluebird' minesweepers with 191 representatives) where lack of space has made it impossible to include all the names with the entry. In most cases a note has been made and all the names will be found in the Index.

The term 'range' used in this book means the distance in nautical miles a ship can run before having to refuel. This has been preferred to 'radius' which is more restrictive, being the distance from a base to sea before having to return to refuel at the same base.

A 'range' entry does not always appear as a number of navies are a little coy about this detail of their ships.

I hope that this, the first of a series of Jane's Pocket Books, will be of value to naval people, press correspondents and the general public who, whether knowingly or not, are intimately affected by the maritime forces of the world's navies and the balance which exists between them.

J. E. MOORE

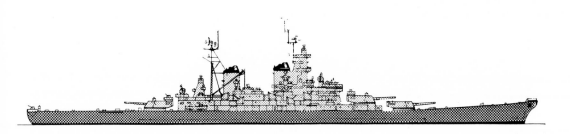

887·2	660	444	221	FEET
270·4	203	135	68	METRES 0

Displacement, tons: 45 000 standard, 59 000 full load
Dimensions, metres: 270·4 × 33 × 11·6 (887·2 × 108·2 × 38 ft)
Aircraft: Can operate helicopters
Guns: 9—16 inch, 20—5 inch

Main machinery: 4 geared turbines, 212 000 shp; 4 shafts
Speed, knots: 33
Complement: Max 2 860
Building dates: 1940-44

NOTES: *Included more as a tribute to the dying mammoths than for its utility. All in reserve with USN—Iowa, New Jersey, Missouri, Wisconsin.*

TYPE: AIRCRAFT CARRIER (HELICOPTER)   CLASS: 'COLOSSUS' ARGENTINA
BRAZIL
FRANCE

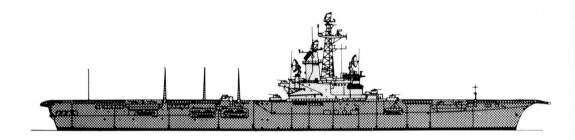

693·2	520	347	178	FEET
211·7	160	106	54	METRES 0

Displacement, tons: 15 890 standard, 19 890 full load
Dimensions, metres: 211·7 × 24·5 × 7 (693·2 × 80 × 23 ft)
Aircraft: 24 helicopters
Main machinery: Parsons geared turbines, 40 000 shp; 2 shafts

Speed, knots: 23·5
Complement: 1 019
Range: 12 000 at 14 knots
Building dates: 1942-45
Special features: All ships' dimensions vary slightly

NOTES: Currently in service in: France (1) Arromanches (transferred from UK 1946); Argentina (1) 25 De Mayo (transferred from UK to Netherlands 1948 and to Argentina 1968); Brazil (1) Minas Gerais (transferred from UK 1956).

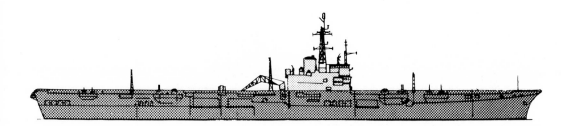

700	523	348	175	FEET
213·4	161	107	54	METRES 0

Displacement, tons: 12 569 standard, 17 233 full load (*Sydney*); 16 000 standard, 19 500 full load (*Vikrant*)

Dimensions, metres: 213·4 × 24·4 × 7·5 (700 × 80 × 25 ft)

Aircraft: 21 capacity (*Vikrant*)

Guns: 15—40 mm AA, 4 twin, 7 single (*Vikrant*); 4—40 mm (*Sydney*)

Main machinery: Parsons single reduction geared turbines, 40 000 shp; 2 shafts

Speed, knots: 24·5 designed

Complement: 1 343 (*Vikrant*); 600 (*Sydney*)

Building dates: 1943-61

NOTES: Currently in service in: Australia (1) Sydney; *India (1)* Vikrant. **Sydney** *is now flagship of the RAN Training Squadron and also used as a transport.* Melbourne *similar.*

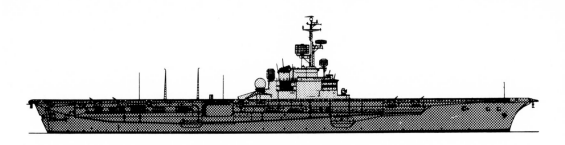

869·4	650	435	214	FEET
265	198	132	66	METRES 0

Displacement, tons: 27 307 normal, 32 800 full load
Dimensions, metres: 265 × 31·7 × 7·7 (869·4 × 104·1 × 25·3 ft)
Aircraft: Capacity 40
Guns: 8—3·9 in (100 mm) AA automatic in single turrets

Main machinery: 2 sets Parsons geared turbines, 126 000 shp; 2 shafts
Speed, knots: 31 max, 24 sustained
Complement: 2 239
Range: 7 500 at 18 knots
Building dates: 1955-63

NOTES: Currently in service in: France (2) Clemenceau, Foch.

737·8	553	369	184	FEET
224·9	168	112	56	METRES 0

Displacement, tons: 23 300 standard, 27 705 full load
Dimensions, metres: 224·9 × 27·4 × 8·5 (737·8 × 90 × 28 ft)
Aircraft: 20 helicopters
Missiles: 2 rocket launchers
Guns: 8—40 mm AA, 4 twin

Main machinery: Parsons geared turbines, 76 000 shp; 2 shafts
Speed, knots: 28
Complement: Approx 1 850 (including embarked commando)
Building dates: 1944-54

NOTES: Of the modified 'Centaur' class converted 1959-62. In service in: UK (2) Albion, Bulwark.

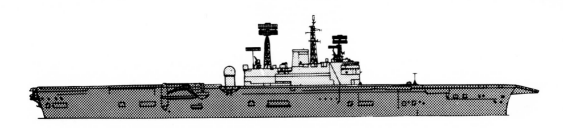

845	633	422	211	FEET
257·6	193	129	64	METRES 0

Displacement, tons: 43 060 standard, 50 786 full load
Dimensions, metres: 257·6 × 34·4 × 11 (845 × 112·8 × 36 ft)
Aircraft: 30 fixed wing + 6 helicopters
Missile launchers: Fitted for four quad Seacat

Main machinery: Parsons single reduction geared turbines, 152 000 shp; 4 shafts
Speed, knots: 31·5 designed max
Complement: 2 640 (as flagship with air crew)
Building dates: 1943-55

NOTES: Modernized from 1967 to 1970.   In service in: UK.

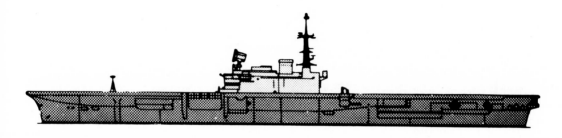

744·3	558	372	186	FEET 0
226·9	178	114	57	METRES

Displacement, tons : 23 900 standard, 28 700 full load
Dimensions, metres : 226·9 × 27·4 × 8·8 (744·3 × 90 × 29 ft)
Aircraft : 20 helicopters
Missiles : 2 quad Seacat surface-to-air systems

Main machinery : Parsons geared turbines, 76 000 shp ; 2 shafts
Speed, knots : 28 designed max
Complement : 2 100 (with air crew)
Building dates : 1944-59

NOTES: Is at present undergoing conversion from a fixed-wing aircraft carrier to the commando ship role. In service in: UK.

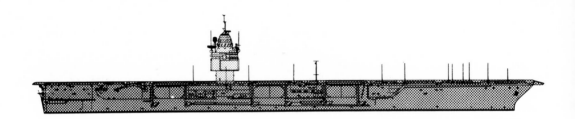

1123	828	552	276	FEET
342·3	255	170	85	METRES 0

Displacement, tons: .75 700 standard, 89 600 full load
Dimensions, metres: 342·3 × 40·5 × 10·8 (1 123 × 133 × 35·8 ft)
Aircraft: 90+
Missiles: 3 Short Range Missile System launchers with Sea Sparrow missiles

Main machinery: 8 A2W nuclear reactors with 4 geared steam turbines (Westinghouse), approx 280 000 shp; 4 shafts
Speed, knots: 35
Complement: 5 500 including air personnel
Building dates: 1958-61

NOTES: In service in: USA.

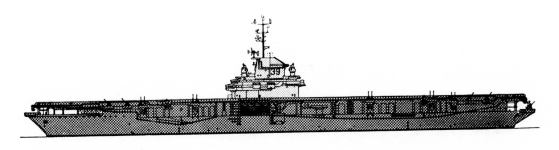

894·5	671	447	224	FEET
273	204	136	68	METRES 0

Displacement, tons: Approx 33 000 standard, 42 000-44 700 full load

Dimensions, metres: Approx 273 × 31·4 × 9·4 (894·5 × 103 × 31 ft)

Aircraft: 45 including 16-18 helicopters ('Essex' class); 45-80 ('Hancock' class)

Guns: 4—5 in (127 mm) dp (single)

Main machinery: 4 geared turbines (Westinghouse), 150 000 shp; 4 shafts

Speed, knots: 33

Complement: 2 400-3 630 (including air crew) ('Hancock' class)

Building dates: 1941-46

NOTES: In service in: USA (14) Antietam, Essex, Yorktown, Hornet, Randolph, Bennington, Kearsage ('Essex' class), Intrepid, Ticonderoga, Lexington, Hancock, Bon Homme Richard, Oriskany, Shangri La ('Hancock' class). 'Hancock' class is modernized version of 'Essex' class.

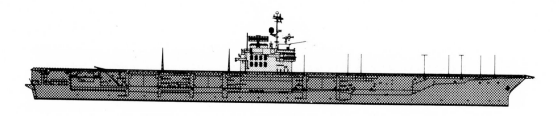

1039	748	519	259	FEET
316·8	228	158	79	0 METRES

Displacement, tons: 63 000 standard, 78 000 full load
Dimensions, metres: 316·8 × 39·5 × 11·3 (1 039 × 129·5 × 37 ft)
Aircraft: 80
Missiles: Sea Sparrow launcher in *Forrestal*
Guns: 4—5 in (127 mm) dp in all but *Forrestal*

Main machinery: 4 geared turbines (Westinghouse), approx 280 000 shp; 4 shafts
Speed, knots: Approx 34-35
Complement: Approx 4 940 (including air crew)
Building dates: 1952-59

NOTES: Currently in service in: USA (4) Forrestal, Saratoga, Ranger, Independence.

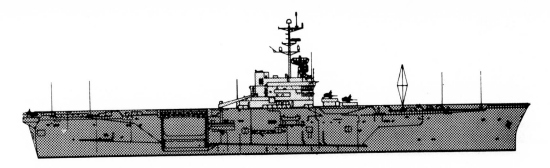

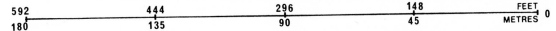

592	444	296	148	FEET
180	135	90	45	METRES 0

Displacement, tons: 17 000 light, 18 300 full load
Dimensions, metres: 180 × 25·6 × 7·9 (592 × 84 × 26 ft)
Aircraft: Approx 30 helicopters
Missiles: 1 Basic Point Defence Missile System (*Okinawa*)

Guns: 8—3 in (76 mm) AA (twin) (6 in *Okinawa*)
Main machinery: 1 geared turbine, 23 000 shp; 1 shaft
Speed, knots: 20 (sustained)
Complement: 528 plus 2 090 troops
Building dates: 1959-70

*NOTES: In service in: USA (7)—known as Amphibious Assault Ships (LPH). Names—*Iwo Jima, Okinawa, Guadalcanal, Guam, Tripoli, New Orleans, Inchon. *The first class ever to be designed primarily for this function.*

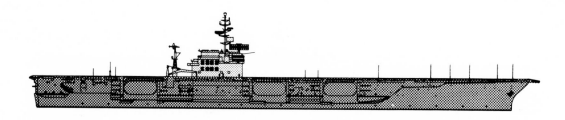

1062·5	797	531	266	FEET
324	245	162	81	METRES 0

Displacement, tons: 60 100 standard, 80 800 full load
 (*JFK* 87 000)
Dimensions, metres: Approx 324 × 39·6 × 11(1 062·5 ×
 130 × 35·9 ft)
Aircraft: 80 to 90
Missiles: 2 twin Terrier surface-to-air launchers, except
JFK, with 3 Sea Sparrow launchers

Main machinery: 4 geared turbines (Westinghouse),
 280 000 shp; 4 shafts
Speed, knots: 35
Complement: 4 950 (including air crew)
Building dates: 1956-68

NOTES: Generally referred to as improved 'Forrestals'; island smaller and further aft. Currently in service in: USA (4)
Kitty Hawk, Constellation, America, J F Kennedy.

979	735	490	245	FEET
298·4	226	149	75	METRES 0

Displacement, tons: Approx 51 500 standard, 64 000 full load

Dimensions, metres: 298·4 × 36·9 × 10·8 (979 × 121 × 35·3 ft)

Aircraft: 75

Guns: 3 or 4—5 in (127 mm) dp

Main machinery: 4 geared turbines, 212 000 shp; 4 shafts

Speed, knots: 33

Complement: Approx 4 450 (including air crew)

Building dates: 1943-47

NOTES: *Have undergone extensive modernization (1953-60). In service in: USA (3)* Midway, F D Roosevelt, Coral Sea.

**TYPE: BALLISTIC MISSILE
SUBMARINE**

CLASS: 'LE REDOUTABLE' FRANCE

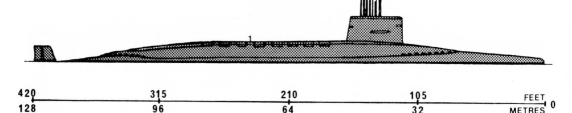

Displacement, tons: 7 500 surface, 9 000 dived
Dimensions, metres: 128 × 10·6 × 10 (420 × 34·8 × 32·8 ft)
Missiles: 16 ICBM; range 1 300 miles
Torpedo tubes: 4 bow 21·7 in (18 torpedoes carried)
Main machinery: 1 pressurized water-cooled reactor;

2 turbo-alternators; 1 motor, 15 000 hp; 1 shaft (auxiliary diesel)
Speed, knots: 20 surface, 25 dived
Complement: 142 (2 crews)
Building dates: 1964, continuing

NOTES: *Currently in service in: France* Le Redoutable, Le Terrible, Le Foudroyant, L'Indomptable. *Last two due to be completed in 1974 and 1976.* Le Tonnant *due for building 1974-78.*

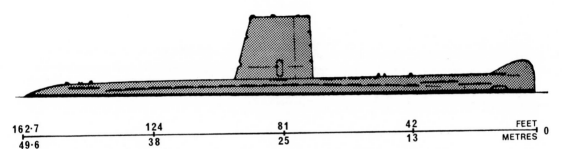

| 162·7 | 124 | 81 | 42 | FEET 0 |
| 49·6 | 38 | 25 | 13 | METRES |

Displacement, tons: 543 surface, 669 dived
Dimensions, metres: 49·6×5·8×4 (162·7 × 19 × 13·1ft)
Torpedo tubes: 4 bow 21·7 in
Mines: All capable of minelaying
Main machinery: Diesel electric, 1 060 hp surface, 1 300
  dived; 1 shaft

Speed, knots: 16 surface, 18 dived
Complement: 40
Building dates: 1955-60

NOTES: Currently in service in: France (*4*) Amazone, Aréthuse, Argonaut, Ariane.

TYPE: PATROL SUBMARINE   **CLASS: 'DAPHNÉ' FRANCE and others**

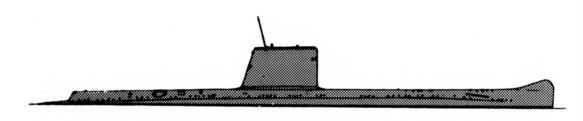

189·6	143	95	47	FEET
57·8	44	29	15	METRES 0

Displacement, tons: 869 surface, 1 043 dived
Dimensions, metres: 57·8 × 6·8 × 4·6 (189·6 × 22·3 × 15·1 ft)
Torpedo tubes: 8 bow, 4 stern, 21·7 in
Mines: All capable of minelaying

Main machinery: Diesel electric, 1 300 bhp surface, 1 600 dived; 2 shafts
Speed, knots: 13·5 surface, 16 dived
Complement: 45
Building dates: 1959-70

NOTES: Currently in service in: France (9), South Africa (3), Pakistan (3), Portugal (4).   See Index for names.

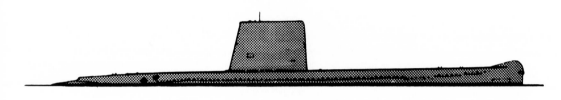

257·2	190	128	64	FEET 0
78·4	59	39	20	METRES

Displacement, tons: 1 640 surface, 1 910 dived
Dimensions, metres: 78·4 × 7·8 × 5·6 (257·2 × 25·6 × 18·5 ft)
Torpedo tubes: 6 bow 21·7 in (20 torpedoes carried)
Mines: All capable of minelaying
Main machinery: 3 Pielstick diesels, 2 motors, 4 800 hp; 2 shafts

Speed, knots: 16 surface, 18 dived
Complement: 67
Range: 15 000 at 8 knots snorting
Building dates: 1950-58

NOTES: Currently in service in: France (6) Marsouin, Narval, Dauphin, Requin, Espadon, Morse.

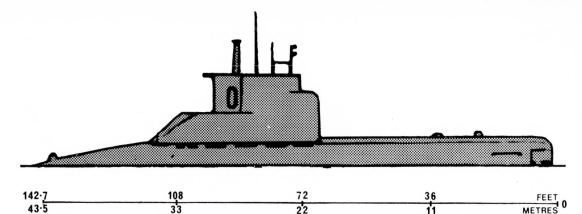

142·7		108		72		36		FEET
43·5		33		22		11		METRES 0

Displacement, tons: 370 surface, 450 dived
Dimensions, metres: 43·5 × 4·6 × 4·3 (142·7 × 15·1 × 13·5 ft)
Torpedo tubes: 8 bow tubes
Mines: All capable of minelaying

Main machinery: 2 Maybach diesels, 1 200 bhp; 2 motors, 1 700 bhp; 1 shaft
Speed, knots: 10 surface, 17 dived
Complement: 18-21

NOTES: Norwegian 'Kobben' class similar—without bulge in forward part of fin and capable of deeper diving Currently in service in: West Germany (11) (numbered from U 1 onwards—U 3 paid off 1963); 12 more o. similar type 206 (U 13-24) due for completion in 1972-73.

TYPE: PATROL SUBMARINE

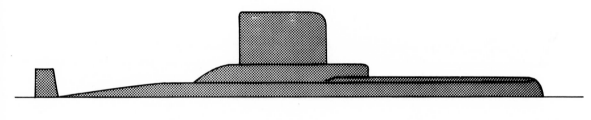

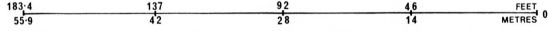

183·4	137	92	46	FEET
55·9	42	28	14	METRES 0

Displacement, tons: 1 000 surface, 1 290 dived
Dimensions, metres: 55·9 × 6·25 × 6 (183·4 × 20·5 × 19·8 ft)
Torpedo tubes: 8—21 inch bow tubes
Mines: Capable of laying mines

Main machinery: Diesel electric, 5 000 hp; 1 shaft
Speed, knots: 22 dived
Complement: 32
Building dates: Launched 1970-71 to enter service 1972-73

NOTES: *Entering service in: Greece (4) Glavkos, Nireus, Proteus, Triton.* Built by Howaldtswerke Deutsche Werft AG, Kiel. *Also building for Argentina, Colombia, Peru and Turkey.*

TYPE: PATROL SUBMARINE   **CLASS: 'TOTI' ITALY**

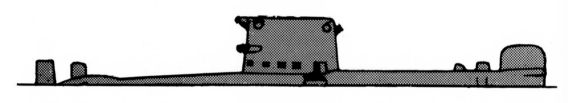

153·2   112   75   39   FEET
46·7   35   23   12   METRES 0

Displacement, tons: 524 surface, 582 dived
Dimensions, metres: 46·7 × 4·7 × 4 (153·2 × 15·4
   × 13·1 ft)
Torpedo tubes: 4 bow 21 in
Main machinery: 4 Fiat diesels, 1 motor (diesel
   electric), 2 200 hp; 1 shaft

Speed, knots: 9 surface, 14 dived
Complement: 24
Range: 6 000 at 5 knots
Building dates: 1965-69

NOTES: Currently in service in: Italy (4) Toti, Bagnolini, Dandolo, Mocenigo. The first post-war Italian submarine construction.

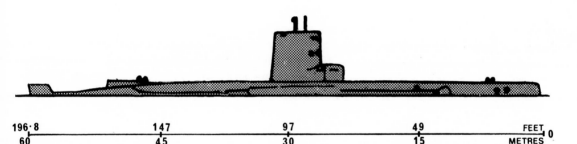

| 196·8 | 147 | 97 | 49 | FEET 0 |
| 60 | 45 | 30 | 15 | METRES |

Displacement, tons: 750 standard
Dimensions, metres: 60 × 6·5 × 4·1 (196·8 × 21·3 × 13·5 ft)
Torpedo tubes: 3 bow 21 in
Main machinery: 2 diesels, 1 350 hp; 2 motors, 1 700 hp; 2 shafts

Speed, knots: 11 surface, 14 dived
Complement: 40
Building dates: 1961-63

NOTES: *Currently in service in: Japan* (*4*) Hayashio, Wakashio, Natsushio, Fuyushio.

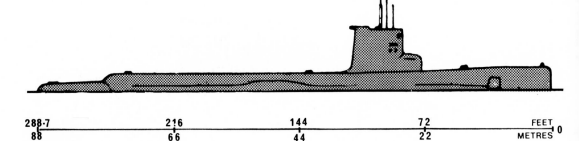

288·7	216	144	72	FEET
88	66	44	22	0 METRES

Displacement, tons: 1 650 standard
Dimensions, metres: 88 × 8·2 × 4·9 (288·7 × 26·9 × 16·2 ft)
Torpedo tubes: 6 bow, 2 stern, 21 in
Mines: All capable of minelaying

Main machinery: 2 diesels, 2 900 bhp; 2 motors, 6 300 hp; 2 shafts
Speed, knots: 14 surface, 18 dived
Complement: 80
Building dates: 1963-69

NOTES: Currently in service in: Japan (5) Oshio, Asashio, Harushio, Michishio, Arashio.

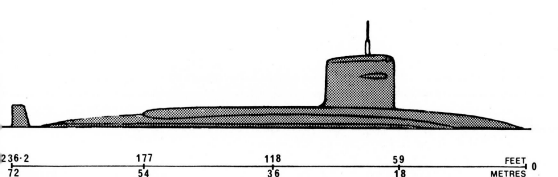

236·2   177   118   59   FEET 0
72   54   36   18   METRES

Displacement, tons: 1 850 standard
Dimensions, metres: 72 × 9·9 × 7·5 (236·2 × 32·5 × 24·6 ft)
Torpedo tubes: 6 bow 21 in
Main machinery: 2 diesels, 3 400 bhp; 1 electric motor, 7 200 hp; 1 shaft

Speed, knots: 12 surface, 20 dived
Complement: 80
Building dates: 1968, continuing

NOTES: Currently in service in: Japan (3) Uzushio, Isoshio, Makishio; 2 more building.

260·9	195	130	65	FEET
79·5	60	40	20	METRES 0

Displacement, tons: 1 494 surface, 1 826 dived
Dimensions, metres: 79·5 × 7·8 × 4·8 (260·9 × 25·8 × 15·8 ft)
Torpedo tubes: 8 bow 21 in
Main machinery: 2 MAN diesels, 3 100 bhp; motors, 4 200 hp; 2 shafts

Speed, knots: 14·5 surface, 17 dived
Complement: 64
Building dates: 1962-66

NOTES: *Currently in service in: Netherlands (*2 *in each class*) Potvis, Tonijn, Dolfijn, Zeehond. *The two classes are similar, both being of the Dutch triple-hulled design.*

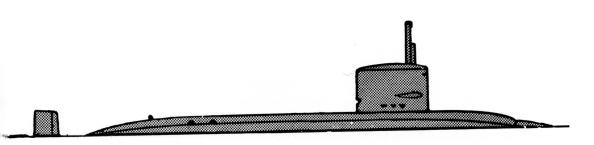

213·3	162	107	54	FEET 0
65	50	33	17	METRES

Displacement, tons: 2 200 surface, 2 650 dived
Dimensions, metres: 65 × 8·4 × 7·1 (213·3 × 27·5 × 23·3 ft)
Torpedo tubes: 6 bow 21 in

Main machinery: Diesel electric, 1 shaft
Speed, knots: 12 surface, 20 dived
Complement: 67
Building dates: 1965-72

NOTES: *Currently in service in: Netherlands* (2) Zwaardvis, Tijgerhaai.

CLASS: 'DRAKEN' SWEDEN

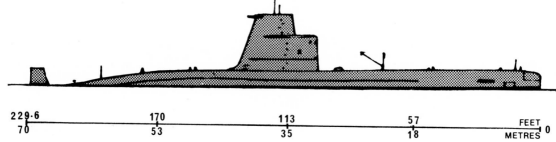

229·6	170	113	57	FEET
70	53	35	18	METRES 0

Displacement, tons: 770 surface, 835 dived
Dimensions, metres: 70 × 5·1 × 5·3 (229·6 × 16·7 × 17·4 ft)
Torpedo tubes: 4 bow 21 in

Main machinery: Diesels/electric motors
Speed, knots: 16·8 surface, 25 dived
Complement: 36
Building dates: 1960-62

NOTES: Currently in service in: Sweden (6) Vargen, Draken, Nordkaparen, Gripen, Delfinen, Springaren.

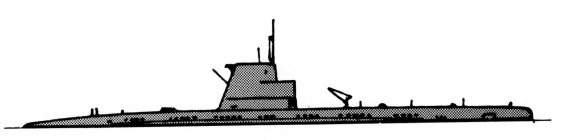

211·6	162	10 6	5 4	FEET 0
64·5	4 8	3 2	16	METRES

Displacement, tons: 785 surface
Dimensions, metres: 64·5 × 5·1 × 4·5 (211·6 × 16·7 × 14·8 ft)
Guns: 1—20 mm
Torpedo tubes: 4 bow 21 in (8 torpedoes carried)

Main machinery: Diesel electric, 1 700 bhp
Speed, knots: 16 surface, 20 dived
Complement: 44
Building dates: 1954-60

NOTES: Currently in service in: Sweden (6) Hajen, Bävern, Illern, Valen, Sälen, Uttern.

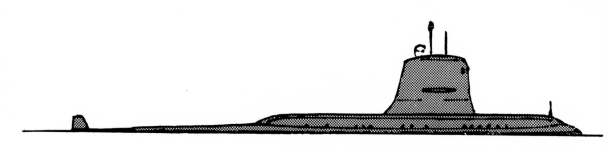

167·3	126	84	43	FEET	0
51	38	25	13	METRES	

Displacement, tons: 800 surface, 1 110 dived
Dimensions, metres: 51 × 6·1 × 6 (167·3 × 20 × 19·7 ft)
Torpedo tubes: 21 in

Main machinery: Diesels/electric motors, 1 shaft
Complement: 23
Building dates: 1967-69

NOTES: Currently in service in: Sweden (5) Sjöormen, Sjölejonet, Sjöhunden, Sjöhästen, Sjöbjörnen.

425	318	212	106	FEET 0
129·5	9 8	6 5	3 3	METRES 0

Displacement, tons: 7 500 surface, 8 400 dived
Dimensions, metres: 129·5 × 10·1 × 9·1 (425 × 33 × 30 ft)
Missiles: 16 Polaris tubes
Torpedo tubes: 6 bow 21 in

Main machinery: Pressurized water-cooled reactor with geared steam turbines; 1 shaft
Speed, knots: 20 surface, 25 dived
Complement: 141 (2 crews)
Building dates: 1964-69

NOTES: Currently in service in: *UK* (*4*) Resolution, Repulse, Renown, Revenge.

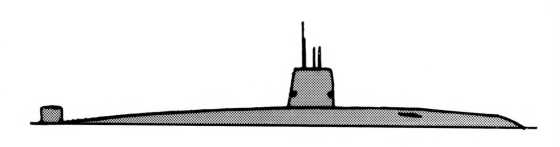

285   213   142   71   FEET 0
86·9   65   43   22   METRES 0

Displacement, tons: 3 500 surface, 4 500 dived
Dimensions, metres: 86·9 × 10·1 × 8·2 (285 × 33·2
  × 27 ft)
Torpedo tubes: 6 bow 21 in
Main machinery: 1 pressurized water-cooled reactor
  with geared steam turbines; 1 shaft

Speed, knots: Approx 30
Complement: 103 (earlier boats), 97 (*Swiftsure* and
  later)
Building dates: 1967, continuing

NOTES: Includes 'Swiftsure' class.   Currently in service in: UK (8) Valiant, Warspite, Churchill, Conqueror, Courageous,
Swiftsure, Sovereign, Superb.

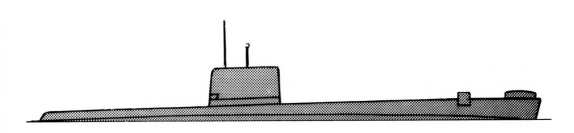

295·2	2 2 1	147	74	FEET
90	6 7	45	2 2	METRES 0

Displacement, tons: 2 030 surface, 2 410 dived
Dimensions, metres: 90 × 8·1 × 5·5 (295·2 × 26 5 × 18 ft)
Torpedo tubes: 6 bow, 2 stern, 21 in
Mines: All capable of minelaying

Main machinery: 2 ASR1 diesels, 3 680 bhp; 2 electric motors, 6 000 shp; 2 shafts
Speed, knots: 12 surface, 17 dived
Complement: 68
Building dates: 1957-63

NOTES: Currently in service in: Australia (4), Brazil (2), Chile (2), Canada (3), UK (13).   UK 'Porpoise' class similar. See Index for names.

TYPE: BALLISTIC MISSILE SUBMARINE   **CLASS: 'ETHAN ALLEN' USA**

410·5	307	205	102	FEET 0
125·1	93	62	31	METRES

Displacement, tons: 6 900 surface, 7 900 dived
Dimensions, metres: 125·1 × 10·1 × 9·4 (410·5 ×
   33 × 30 ft)
Missiles: 16 Polaris tubes
Torpedo tubes: 4 bow 21 in

Main machinery: 1 pressurized water-cooled S5W
   reactor; 1 geared turbine, 15 000 shp; 1 shaft
Speed, knots: 20 surface, approx 30 dived
Complement: 112 (2 crews)
Building dates: 1959-63

NOTES: Currently in service in: USA (5) Ethan Allen, Sam Houston, Thomas A Edison. John Marshall, Thomas Jefferson.

381·7	286	191	95	FEET
116·4	87	58	29	METRES 0

Displacement, tons: 5 900 surface, 6 700 dived
Dimensions, metres: 116·4 × 10·1 × 8·8 (381·7 × 33 × 29 ft)
Missiles: 16 Polaris tubes
Torpedo tubes: 6 bow 21 in
Main machinery: 1 pressurized water-cooled S5W reactor; 1 geared turbine, 15 000 shp; 1 shaft

Speed, knots: 20 surface, approx 30 dived
Complement: 112 (2 crews)
Building dates: 1959-61
Special features: Distinctive silhouette caused by high after-casing around missile tubes

NOTES: *Currently in service in: USA* (5) George Washington, Patrick Henry, Robert E Lee, Theodore Roosevelt, Abraham Lincoln.

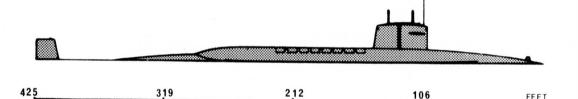

425	319	212	106	FEET
129·5	98	65	33	METRES 0

Displacement, tons: 7 320 surface, 8 250 dived
Dimensions, metres: 129·5 × 10·1 × 9·6 (425 × 33 × 31·5 ft)
Missiles: 16 Polaris tubes
Torpedo tubes: 4 bow 21 in

Main machinery: 1 pressurized water-cooled S5W reactor; 2 geared turbines, 15 000 shp; 1 shaft
Speed, knots: 20 surface, approx 30 dived
Complement: 140 (2 crews)
Building dates: 1961-67

NOTES: Currently in service in: USA (31). See Index for names. First three fitted for A2 missiles, remainder for A3. 20 are due for conversion to Poseidon.

278·5	209	139	70	FEET	0
84·9	64	42	21	METRES	

Displacement, tons: 3 750 surface, 4 300 dived
Dimensions, metres: 84·9 × 9·6 × 7·6 (278·5 × 31·7
  × 25·2 ft)
Torpedo tubes: 4 amidships, 21 in, with SUBROC
Main machinery: 1 pressurized water-cooled S5W
  reactor; 2 steam turbines, 15 000 shp: 1 shaft

Speed, knots: Approx 20 surface, 30 dived
Complement: 107
Building dates: 1959-67

NOTES: *Currently in service in: USA (13)* Flasher, Greenling *and* Gato *slightly larger than others;* Permit, Plunger,
Barb, Pollack, Haddo, Dace, Tinosa, Guardfish, Jack, Haddock.

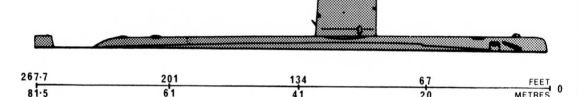

267·7	201	134	67	FEET
81·5	61	41	20	METRES 0

Displacement, tons: 2 570 surface, 2 861 dived
Dimensions, metres: 81·5 × 7·6 × 6·4 (267·7 × 25 × 21 ft)
Torpedo tubes: 4 bow, 2 stern, 21 in
Main machinery: 1 pressurized water-cooled S3W or S4W reactor; 2 steam turbines, 6 600 hp; 2 shafts

Speed, knots: 20 surface, approx 25 dived
Complement: 95
Building dates: 1955-59

NOTES: Currently in service in: USA (4) Skate, Swordfish, Sargo, Seadragon.

251·7   189   126   63   FEET 0
76·7   58   38   19   METRES

Displacement, tons: 3 075 surface, 3 500 dived
Dimensions, metres: 76·7 × 9·6 × 8·5 (251·7 × 31·5 × 28 ft)
Torpedo tubes: 6 bow 21 in
Main machinery: 1 pressurized water-cooled S5W reactor; 2 steam turbines, 15 000 shp; 1 shaft

Speed, knots: Approx 20 surface, 30 dived
Complement: 93
Building dates: 1956-61

NOTES: Currently in service in: USA (5) Skipjack, Scamp, Sculpin, Shark, Snook.

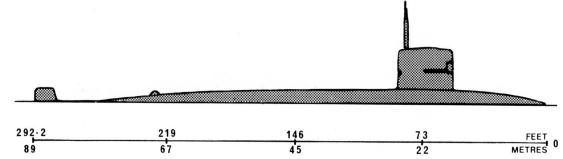

292·2	219	146	73	FEET
89	67	45	22	METRES 0

Displacement, tons: 3 860 surface, 4 630 dived
Dimensions, metres: 89 × 9·5 × 7·9 (292·2 × 31·7 × 26 ft)
Torpedo tubes: 4 amidships, 21 in, with SUBROC
Main machinery: 1 pressurized water-cooled S5W reactor; 2 steam turbines, 15 000 shp; 1 shaft

Speed, knots: Approx 20 surface, 30 dived
Complement: 107
Building dates: 1963, continuing

NOTES: Currently in service in: USA (37). See Index for names.

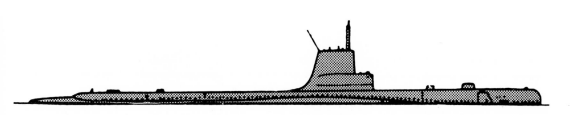

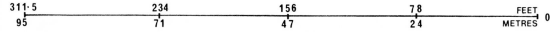

311·5	234	156	7 8	FEET
95	71	47	2 4	METRES 0

Displacement, tons: 1 829 surface, 2 424 dived
Dimensions, metres: 95 × 8·3 × 4·2 (311·5 × 27 × 13·8 ft)
Guns: Originally 1—5 in, generally removed
Torpedo tubes: 6 bow, 4 stern, 21 in (24 torpedoes carried)
Mines: All capable of minelaying

Main machinery: 4 GM diesels, 6 500 hp; 2 motors, 2 750 hp
Speed, knots: 20 surface, 10 dived
Complement: 85
Range: 12 000 at 10 knots surfaced
Building dates: 1944-45

NOTES: Currently in service in: Turkey (8), Italy (3), Spain (1), Greece (1), Chile (1), Venezuela (1). See Index for names.

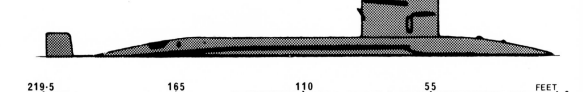

219·5	165	110	55	FEET
66·8	50	33	17	METRES 0

Displacement, tons: 2 145 surface, 2 895 dived
Dimensions, metres: 66·8 × 8·8 × 8·5 (219·5 × 29 × 28 ft)
Torpedo tubes: 6 bow 21 in
Main machinery: 3 diesels, 4 800 hp; GE motors; 1 shaft

Speed, knots: 15 surface, 25 dived
Complement: 79
Building dates: 1956-59

NOTES: *Currently in service in: USA* (3) *Barbel, Bonefish, Blueback. The last USN conventional operational submarines with a 'tear-drop' hull formation.*

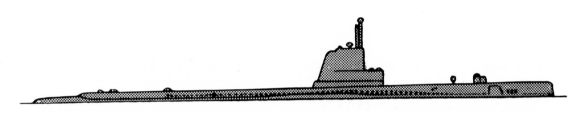

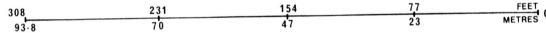

308	231	154	77	FEET 0
93·8	70	47	23	METRES

Displacement, tons, 1 870 surface, 2 440 dived
Dimensions, metres: 93·8 × 8·2 × 5·2 (308 × 27 × 17 ft)
Torpedo tubes: 6 bow, 4 stern, 21 in
Mines: All capable of minelaying
Main machinery: 3 diesels, 4 800 hp; 2 motors,
5 400 hp: 2 shafts

Speed, knots: 18 surface, 15 dived
Complement: 84
Building dates: 1944, converted 1951

NOTES: Currently in service in: USA (5) Becuna, Atule, Blenny, Sea Poacher, Tench; Argentina (1) Santiago del Estero; Greece (1) ex-Blackfin; Turkey (1) Dumlupinar. Some still have stepped fins as shown—remainder are similar to Guppy IIA.

TYPE: PATROL SUBMARINE   **CLASS: 'GUPPY II' USA and others**

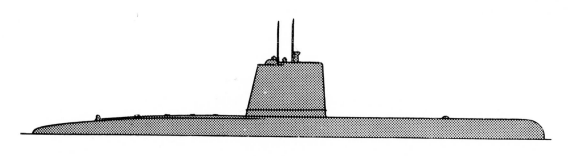

307·5	231	154	77	FEET
93·6	70	47	23	METRES 0

Displacement, tons: 1 870 surface, 2 420 dived
Dimensions, metres: 93·6 × 8·3 × 5·5 (307·5 × 27·2 × 18 ft)
Torpedo tubes: 6 bow, 4 stern, 21 in
Mines: All capable of minelaying

Main machinery: 3 diesels, 4 800 shp; 2 motors, 5 400 shp; 2 shafts
Speed, knots: 18 surface, 15 dived
Complement: 82
Building dates: 1944-51, converted 1948-50

NOTES: Currently in service in: USA (5) Amberjack, Cutlass, Grenadier, Sea Leopard, Tusk; *Argentina*(1) Santa Fe; *Brazil* (3) Guanbara, Rio De Janeiro, Rio Grande Do Sul; *Venezuela* (1) *ex*-Cubera.

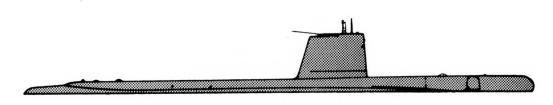

306	231	154	77	FEET
93·2	70	47	23	METRES 0

Displacement, tons: 1 840 surface, 2 445 dived
Dimensions, metres: 93·2 × 8·2 × 5·2 (306 × 27 × 17 ft)
Torpedo tubes: 6 bow, 4 stern, 21 in
Mines: All capable of minelaying

Main machinery: 3 diesels, 4 800 hp; 2 motors, 5 400 hp; 2 shafts
Speed, knots: 18 surface, 15 dived
Complement: 84
Building dates: 1943-45, converted 1952-54

NOTES: Currently in service in: USA (5) Bang, Menhaden, Tirante, Jallao, Quillback; Greece (1) Papanikolis; Spain (2) Isaac Peral, Narciso Monturiol; Turkey (7) Burak Reis, Murat Reis, Oruc Reis, Ulucali Reis, Preveze, Cerbe, ex-Threadfin. A few still have a step in the forward end of the fin.

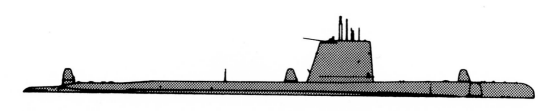

326·5	245	163	82	FEET
99·4	75	50	25	METRES 0

Displacement, tons: 1 975 surface, 2 540 dived
Dimensions, metres: 99·4 × 8·2 × 5·2 (326·5 × 27 × 17 ft)
Torpedo tubes: 6 bow, 4 stern, 21 in
Mines: All capable of minelaying

Main machinery: 4 diesels, 6 400 hp; 2 motors, 5 400 hp; 2 shafts
Speed, knots: 20 surface, 15 dived
Complement: 86
Building dates: 1944-49, modernized 1960-62

NOTES: Currently in service in: USA (7) Clamagore, Cobbler, Corporal, Greenfish, Remora, Tiru, Trumpetfish; *Italy* (2) *ex*-Volador, *ex*-Pickerel. *A comprehensive reconstruction of boats of the 'Tench' and 'Balao' classes to provide greater underwater performance. All Guppys have rounded bows while most streamlined patrol submarines have raked straight bows.*

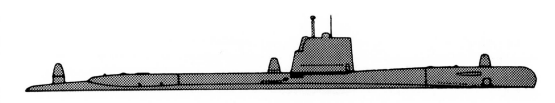

287   215   145   72   FEET 0
87·4   66   44   22   METRES

Displacement, tons: 2 100 surface, 2 700 dived
Dimensions, metres: 87·4 × 8·3 × 6·2 (287 × 27·3 × 19 ft)
Torpedo tubes: 6 bow, 2 stern, 21 in
Main machinery: 3 diesels, 4 500 shp; 2 motors, 5 600 shp; twin screw

Speed, knots: 20 surface, 18 dived
Complement: 83
Building dates: 1949-52

NOTES: *Currently in service in: USA (6)* Tang, Trigger, Wahoo, Trout, Harder, Gudgeon. Trigger *was the first post-war US submarine to be laid down (24 Feb 1949).*

TYPE: BALLISTIC MISSILE SUBMARINE

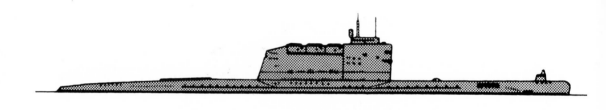

320 — 97·5 | 240 — 73 | 160 — 49 | 80 — 24 | FEET 0 — METRES

Displacement, tons: 2 350 surface, 2 800 dived
Dimensions, metres: 97·5 × 7·6 × 6·7 (320 × 25·1 × 22 ft)
Missiles: 'G1'—3 SSN—4 (300 miles); 'G2'—3 SSN—5 (650 miles)
Torpedo tubes: 10 bow 21 in
Mines: Could be carried but not likely

Main machinery: 3 diesels, 6 000 hp; 3 shafts; electric motors, 6 000 hp
Speed, knots: 17·6 surface, 17 dived
Complement: 86
Range: 22 700 surfaced, cruising
Building dates: From 1958

NOTES: *Currently in service in: USSR (22), China (1). Existence of missiles for the latter is still debatable.*

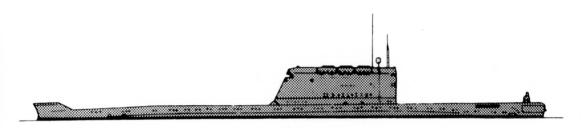

377·2	284	189	95	FEET	0
115·2	87	58	29	METRES	0

Displacement, tons: 3 700 surface, 4 100 dived
Dimensions, metres: 115·2 × 8·6 × 7·6 (377·2 × 28·4 × 25 ft)
Missiles: 3 SSN-5 tubes
Torpedo tubes: 6 bow 21 in; 4 stern 16 in

Mines: Could be carried but unlikely
Main machinery: Nuclear reactor, steam turbine, 22 500 hp
Speed, knots: 20
Complement: 90

NOTES: Currently in service in: USSR (9). Fin-mounted missile tubes.

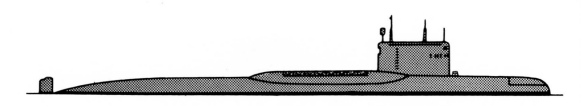

426·5	320	213	106	FEET
130	97	65	33	METRES 0

Displacement, tons: 8 000 surface, 9 000 dived
Dimensions, metres: 130 × 10·6 × 10 (426·5 × 34·8 × 32·8 ft)
Missiles: 16 SSN6 tubes (1 300 miles missile range)
Torpedo tubes: 8 bow 21 in

Mines: Could be carried but unlikely
Main machinery: Nuclear reactors, steam turbines, 60 000 hp
Speed, knots: 25
Building dates: From 1964

NOTES: Currently in service in: USSR (30 by end 1972).

295·3   222   148   74   FEET
| | | | | 0
90   67   45   22   METRES

Displacement, tons: 2 100 surface, 2 600 dived
Dimensions, metres: 90 × 7·3 × 5·8 (295·3 × 24·1 × 19 ft)
Missiles: 2 SSN-4 (300 miles)
Torpedo tubes: 10—21 in
Mines: Could be carried but unlikely

Main machinery: 3 diesels, 3 shafts, 10 000 hp; 3 electric motors, 3 500 hp
Speed, knots: 18 surface, 15 dived
Complement: 85
Special features: Conversion from standard 'Z' class 1956-58

NOTES: Currently in service in: USSR (4).

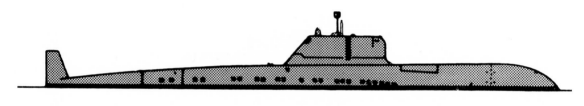

295	222	148	74	FEET
90	68	45	23	METRES 0

Displacement, tons: 4 000 surface, 5 000 dived
Dimensions, metres: 90 × 10 × 7·5 (295 × 32·8 × 24·6 ft)
Missiles: 8 short range (25 miles)
Torpedo tubes: 8 bow 21 in
Mines: Could be carried but unlikely

Main machinery: Nuclear reactors; steam turbines, 24 000 hp
Speed, knots: 30 dived
Complement: 100
Building dates: 1968 onwards

NOTES: Currently in service in: USSR (5).

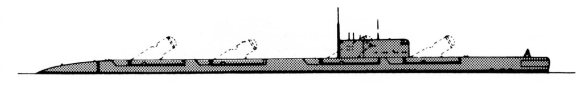

387·4	291	194	97	FEET 0
118	90	59	30	METRES

Displacement, tons: 5 000 surface, 5 600 dived
Dimensions, metres: 118 × 8·6 × 8·3 (387·4 × 28·4 × 27 ft)
Missiles: 8 SSN-3 (Shaddock) (300 miles)
Torpedo tubes: 6 bow 21 in; 4 stern 16 in
Mines: Could be carried but unlikely

Main machinery: Nuclear reactor; steam turbines, 22 500 hp
Speed, knots: 20
Complement: 100
Building dates: From 1963
Special features: Required to surface to fire

NOTES: Currently in service in: USSR (27).

TYPE: CRUISE MISSILE SUBMARINE   **CLASS: 'J' USSR**

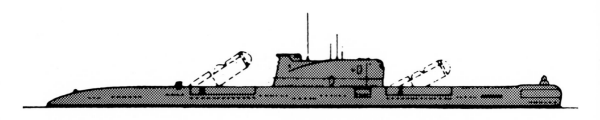

280·5	210	140	70	FEET
85·5	64	43	21	METRES 0

Displacement, tons: 2 200 surface, 2 500 dived
Dimensions, metres: 85·5 × 9·5 × 6·1 (280·5 × 31·4 × 20 ft)
Missiles: 4 SSN-3 (Shaddock) (300 miles)
Torpedo tubes: 6 bow 21 in, 2/4 stern 16 in

Mines: Could be carried but unlikely
Main machinery: Diesels, 6 000 bhp; electric motors, 6 000 bhp
Speed, knots: 16 surface, 16 dived
Building dates: From 1962

NOTES: *Currently in service in: USSR (16).*

| 272·3 | 205 | 136 | 69 | FEET | 0 |
| 83 | 62 | 41 | 21 | METRES | |

Displacement, tons: 1 300 surface, 1 800 dived
Dimensions, metres: 83 × 6 × 4·8 (272·3 × 19·8 × 15·7 ft)
Missiles: 4 SSN-3 (Shaddock) (300 miles)
Torpedo tubes: 4 bow 21 in
Mines: Could be carried but unlikely

Main machinery: Diesels, 4 000 hp; electric motors, 2 500 hp
Speed, knots: 17 surface, 15 dived
Building dates: Converted 1959-63
Special features: 'W' class extended by 10 m with 4 launchers forward in conning tower

NOTES: Currently in service in: USSR (6).

247·5	186	124	62	FEET
75·3	57	38	19	METRES

Displacement, tons: 1 100 surface 1 600 dived
Dimensions, metres: 75·3 × 5·8 × 4·6 (247·5 × 19·1 × 15·1 ft)
Missiles: 2 SSN-3 (Shaddock) (300 miles)
Torpedo tubes: 4 bow 21 in, 2 stern 21 in
Mines: Could be carried but unlikely

Main machinery: Diesels, 4 000 hp; electric motors, 2 500 hp
Speed, knots: 17 surface, 15 dived
Building dates: Converted 1956-60
Special features: 'W' class extended by 8 m with 2 launchers abaft the conning tower

NOTES: Currently in service in: USSR (6).

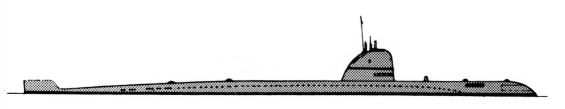

357·7   268   179   89   FEET

109   82   55   28   METRES

Displacement, tons: 3 500 surface, 4 000 dived
Dimensions, metres: 109 × 8·6 × 7·4 (357·7 × 28·2 × 24·3 ft)
Torpedo tubes: 6 bow 21 in, 4 stern 16 in
Mines: Could be carried but unlikely
Main machinery: Nuclear reactor, steam turbines, 22 500 hp

Speed, knots: 20 surface, 25 dived
Complement: 88
Building dates: 1958-65

NOTES: Currently in service in: USSR (13). The first class of Soviet fleet submarines; noisy.

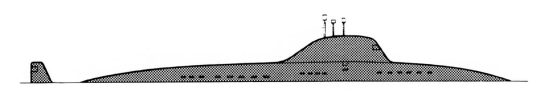

285·4	214	143	71	FEET
87	65	43	22	METRES 0

Displacement, tons: 3 600 surface, 4 200 dived
Dimensions, metres: 87 × 10 × 8 (285·4 × 32·8 × 26·2 ft)
Torpedo tubes: 8 bow 21 in
Mines: Could be carried but unlikely

Main machinery: Nuclear reactor, steam turbines, 30 000 hp
Speed, knots: 26 surface, 31 dived
Complement: About 80
Building dates: 1966, continuing

NOTES: Currently in service in: USSR (7).

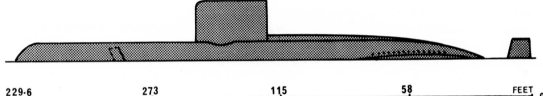

229·6	273	115	58	FEET
70	52	35	17	METRES 0

Displacement, tons: 1 000 surface, 1 100 dived
Dimensions, metres: 70 × 7·5 × 4·5 (229·6 × 24·8
 × 14·8 ft)
Torpedo tubes: 6 bow 21 in
Main machinery: Diesel electric?
Speed, knots: 16?

NOTES: Currently in service in: USSR (6). Details require confirmation. An interesting submarine whose purpose and propulsion are still in doubt.

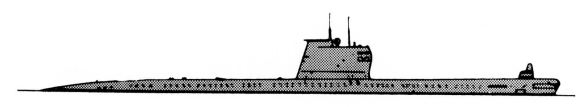

296·8	222	148	74	FEET
90·5	68	45	23	0 METRES

Displacement, tons: 2 000 surface, 2 300 dived
Dimensions, metres: 90·5 × 7·3 × 5·8 (296·8 × 24·1 × 19 ft)
Torpedo tubes: 6 bow 21 in, 4 stern 21 in (20 torpedoes carried)

Main machinery: Diesel, 6 000 bhp: 3 shafts; 3 electric motors, 6 000 hp
Speed, knots: 20 surface, 15 dived
Complement: 70
Building dates: 1956-67

NOTES: Currently in service in: USSR (45), India (4). A very successful design currently much deployed abroad particularly in the Mediterranean.

TYPE: PATROL SUBMARINE

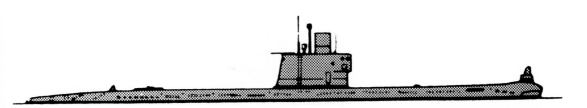

246	184	123	61	FEET
75	56	37	18	METRES	0

Displacement, tons: 1 100 surface, 1 600 dived
Dimensions, metres: 75 × 7·3 × 4·4 (246 × 24 × 14·5 ft)
Torpedo tubes: 6 bow 21 in
Main machinery: Diesels, 4 000 bhp; electric motors, 4 000 hp

Speed, knots: 19 surface, 16 dived
Complement: 65
Building dates: 1958-61

NOTES: Currently in service in: USSR (14), China (14), Egypt (6). An improved form of 'W' class. Now being built in China. High fairing on top of fin is a distinctive feature.

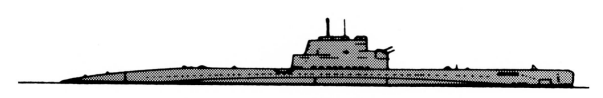

248·5	186	124	62	FEET 0
75·3	55	37	18	METRES

Displacement, tons: 1 030 surface, 1 180 dived
Dimensions, metres: 75·3 × 5·8 × 4·6 (248·5 × 19·1 × 15 ft)
Torpedo tubes: 4 bow 21 in, 2 stern 21 in (18 torpedoes carried)
Mines: 40
Main machinery: 2 diesels, 4 000 hp; electric motors, 2 500 hp; 2 shafts

Speed, knots: 17 surface, 15 dived
Complement: 60
Building dates: 1950-57
Special features: 5 'W' class converted to 'canvas bag' as radar pickets with large, conspicuous bridge aerial

NOTES: *Currently in service in: USSR(148), Albania (4), Bulgaria (2), China (21), Egypt (6), Indonesia (10) and Poland (4).*

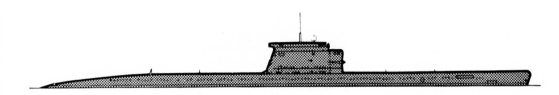

295·3   223   148   75   FEET 0
90   67   45   22   METRES

Displacement, tons: 1 900 surface, 2 200 dived
Dimensions, metres: 90 × 7·3 × 5·8 (295·3 × 23·9
    × 19 ft)
Torpedo tubes: 6 bow 21 in, 4 stern 21 in (24 torpedoes
    carried)
Mines: 40 mines in lieu of torpedoes

Main machinery: Diesel electric; 3 diesels, 10 000 bhp;
    3 shafts; 3 electric motors, 3 500 hp
Speed, knots: 18 surface, 15 dived
Complement: 70
Range: 20 000
Building dates: 1951-57

*NOTES: Currently in service in: USSR (22). The smaller fin with a step in the forward end distinguishes this class
from the ZV conversion.*

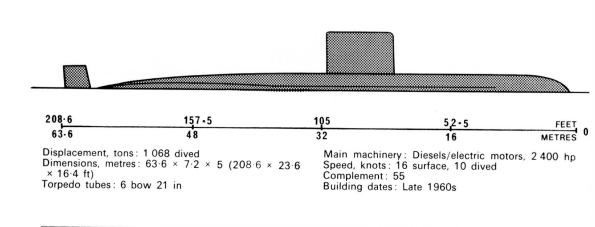

Displacement, tons: 1 068 dived
Dimensions, metres: 63·6 × 7·2 × 5 (208·6 × 23·6 × 16·4 ft)
Torpedo tubes: 6 bow 21 in

Main machinery: Diesels/electric motors, 2 400 hp
Speed, knots: 16 surface, 10 dived
Complement: 55
Building dates: Late 1960s

NOTES: Currently in service in: Yugoslavia (3) Heroj, Junak, Uskok.

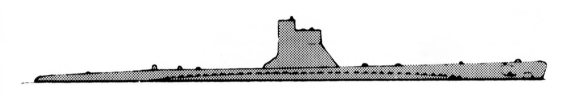

196·8	147·75	98-5	49-25	FEET	0
60	45	30	15	METRES	

Displacement, tons: 945 dived
Dimensions, metres: 60 × 6·8 × 4·9 (196·8 × 22·3 × 16·1 ft)
Torpedo tubes: 6 bow 21 in
Main machinery: Diesels/electric motors, 1 800 hp

Speed, knots: 14 surface, 9 dived
Complement: 38
Range: 9 600 miles at 8 knots
Building dates: 1958-60

NOTES: Currently in service in: Yugoslavia (2) Neretva, Sutjeska. The first submarines to be built in a Yugoslav yard.

TYPE: CRUISER

CLASS: 'BROOKLYN' ARGENTINA
BRAZIL
CHILE
(USA)

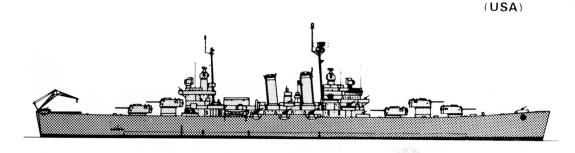

608·3	456	304	152	FEET
185·4	138	92	46	METRES 0

Displacement, tons: Approx 10 650 standard, 13 645
full load
Dimensions, metres: 185·4 × 21 × 7·3 (608·3 × 69
× 24 ft)
Aircraft: 2 helicopters
Missiles, AA: 2 quad Seacat launchers (*General
Belgrano*)
Guns, surface: 15—6 in, 8—5 in

Guns, AA: 28—40 mm, 16—20 mm
Main machinery: Westinghouse geared turbines,
100 000 shp; 4 shafts
Speed, knots: 32·5
Complement: 1 200
Range: 15 000 at 15 knots
Building dates: 1935-39

*NOTES: Reconditioned in 1951 on transfer from USN. In service in: Argentina (2), General Belgrano, Nueve de
Julio; Brazil (1) Barroso; Chile (2) O'Higgins, Prat.*

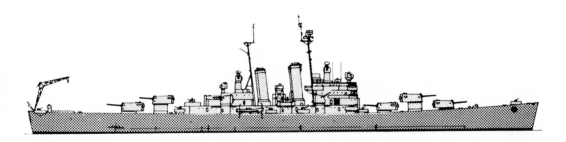

608·5	456	304	152	FEET	0
185·5	138	92	46	METRES	

Displacement, tons: 10 000 standard, 13 500 full load
Dimensions, metres: 185·5 × 21 × 7·3 (608·5 × 69 × 24 ft)
Aircraft: 1 helicopter
Guns: 15—6 in (5 triple), 8—5 in (4 twin), 28—40 mm, 8—20 mm

Main machinery: Westinghouse geared turbines, 100 000 shp; 4 shafts
Speed, knots: 32·5
Complement: 975
Range: 14 500 at 15 knots
Building dates: 1936-39

NOTES: *In service in: Brazil (1) Tamandare. Transferred from USN 1951.*

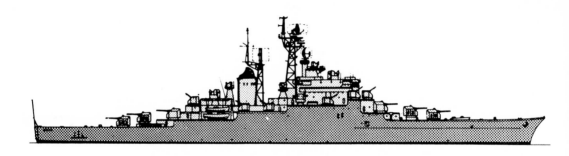

593·2	445	296	148	FEET	
180·8	135	90	45	METRES	0

Displacement, tons: 8 500 standard, 11 300 full load
Dimensions, metres: 180·8 × 19·7 × 7·7 (593·2 × 64·6 × 25·2 ft)
Missile launchers: 1 twin Masurca surface-to-air aft
Guns: 2—3·9 in single automatic, 12—57 mm in 6 twin mountings, 3 on each side

Main machinery: 2 sets CEM-Parsons geared turbines. 86 000 shp; 2 shafts
Speed, knots: 32·4 max
Complement: 800 (as flagship)
Range: 8 000 at 25 knots
Building dates: 1953-58; reconstruction 1970-73

NOTES: In service in: France (1). Colbert *is due to return to the fleet in 1973.*

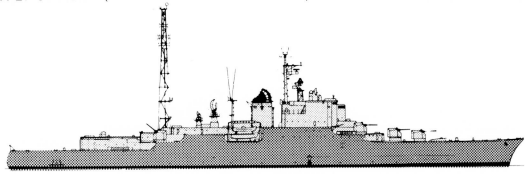

617·8	463	308	154	FEET	
188·3	141	94	47	METRES	0

Displacement, tons: 9 000 standard, 12 350 full load
Dimensions, metres: 188·3 × 21·3 × 6·53 (617·8 × 69·9 × 21·4 ft)
Guns: 12—5 in (6 twin mountings)
Main machinery: 2 sets Rateau-Chantiers de Bretagne geared turbines, 105 000 shp; 2 shafts

Speed, knots: 33 max, 18 cruising
Complement: 560
Range: 5 200 at 18 knots, 2 500 at full power
Building dates: 1938-56

NOTES: Construction was suspended during the German occupation of Lorient. Resumed in 1946 and again held up in 1947-51. In service in: France (1) De Grasse.

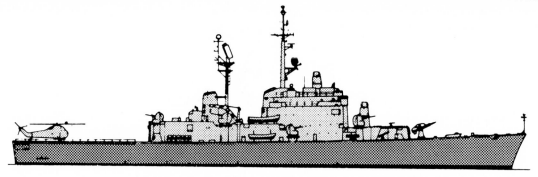

489·8	370	245	122	FEET
149·3	112	75	37	METRES 0

Displacement, tons: 5 000 standard, 6 500 full load
Dimensions, metres: 149·3 × 17·2 × 5 (489·8 × 56·4 × 16·4 ft)
Aircraft: 4 A/B 204 B ASW helicopters
Missiles: 1 Terrier twin launcher forward
Guns: 8—3 in AA (singles)
Torpedo tubes: 2 triple for 12-in A/S torpedoes

Main machinery: 2 double reduction geared turbines, 60 000 shp; 2 shafts
Speed, knots: 31 designed, 30 sustained
Complement: 478
Range: 12 000 at 20 knots
Building dates: 1958-64

NOTES: In service in: Italy (2) Andrea Doria, Caio Duilio.

TYPE: CRUISER (CLG)   CLASS: 'VITTORIO VENETO' ITALY   69

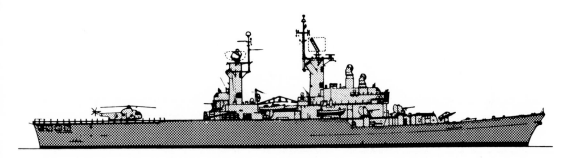

557·7	422	179	142	FEET
170	128	85	43	METRES 0

Displacement, tons: 7 500 standard, 8 850 full load
Dimensions, metres: 170 × 19·4 × 5·2 (557·7 × 63·6 × 17·2 ft)
Aircraft: 9 A/B 240 B ASW helicopters
Missiles: 1 Terrier/ASROC twin launcher forward
Guns: 8—3 in AA
Torpedo tubes: 2 triple for A/S torpedoes

Main machinery: 2 Tosi double reduction geared turbines, 73 000 shp; 2 shafts
Speed, knots: 32 designed
Complement: 530
Range: 12 000 at 20 knots
Building dates: 1965-69

NOTES: In service in: Italy (1) Vittorio Veneto. A development of the 'Andrea Doria' class with more than double her establishment of helicopters for an increase of 2 000 tons (full load) and with a slightly higher speed.

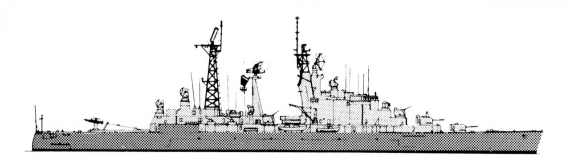

614·5	465	307	155	FEET
187·3	142	94	47	METRES 0

Displacement, tons: 9 529 standard, 11 850 full load

Dimensions, metres: 187·3×17·3 × 6·7 (614·5 × 56·7 × 22 ft)

Missiles, AA: 1 twin Terrier launcher aft in *De Zeven Provincien*

Guns, surface: 8—6 in in twin turrets, 8—57 mm in twin turrets, 8—40 mm (*De Ruyter*); 4—6 in, 6—57 mm, 4—40 mm (*De Zeven Provincien*)

Main machinery: 2 De Schelde-Parsons geared turbines, 85 000 shp; 2 shafts

Speed, knots: 32

Complement: 926-940

Building dates: 1939-53

NOTES: In service in: Netherlands (2) De Ruyter, De Zeven Provincien. *Construction of both held up during the war. Terrier fit in* De Zeven Provincien *carried out 1962-64 and further modernization 1971-72.*

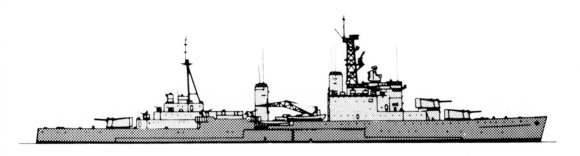

555·5	419	278	139	FEET
169·3	127	85	42	METRES 0

Displacement, tons: Approx 8 790 standard, 11 100
   full load
Dimensions, metres: 169·3 × 19·4 × 5   (555·5 ×
   63·6 × 16·5 ft)
Guns, surface: 9—6 in (152 mm), 3 triple
Guns, dual purpose: 8—4 in (4 twin)
Guns, AA: 12 or 18—40 mm

Main machinery: Parsons geared turbines, 72 500 shp;
   4 shafts
Speed, knots: 31·5
Complement: 743-766
Range: 12 000 at 13 knots
Building dates: 1939-43

*NOTES: Modernized 1951-56. In service in: Peru (2) Almirante Grau, Coronel Bolognesi (ex-UK); India (1)
Mysore.*

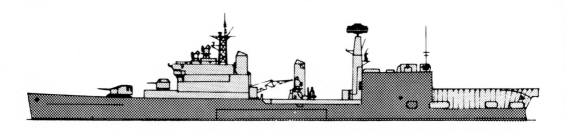

566·5	429	283	142	FEET	0
172·8	130	86	43	METRES	

Displacement, tons: 9 500 standard, 12 080 full load
Dimensions, metres: 172·8 × 19·5 × 7 (566·5 × 64 × 23 ft)
Aircraft: 4 helicopters
Missile launchers: 2 quad Seacat
Guns: 2—6 in (1 twin), 2—3 in (1 twin)

Main machinery: 4 Parsons geared turbines, 80 000 shp; 4 shafts
Speed, knots: 31·5 max
Complement: 885
Range: Approx 4 000 at 20 knots
Building dates: 1941-61

NOTES: In service in: UK (2) Tiger, Blake. Originally a class of 5 conventional cruisers—2 cancelled and Lion disposed of 1972. The 3 built were delayed 8 years from 1946—Blake converted to helicopter cruiser 1965-69, Tiger 1967-72.

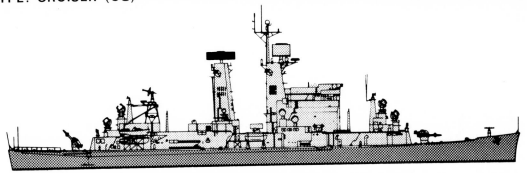

673	508	336	169	FEET	0
205·2	154	103	51	METRES	

Displacement, tons: 13 700 standard, 17 500 full load
Dimensions, metres: 205·2 × 21·3 × 8·2 (673×69·9 × 26·9 ft)
Aircraft: Utility helicopter carried
Missiles: 2 twin Talos surface-to-air launchers, 2 twin Tartar surface-to-air launchers
Guns: 2—5 in dp (single)

A/S weapons: 1 ASROC 8-tube launcher, 2 triple torpedo launchers
Main machinery: 4 geared turbines (General Electric), 120 000 shp; 4 shafts
Speed, knots: 33
Complement: 1 000
Building dates: 1943-46

NOTES: Converted from conventional cruisers 1959-64, and modernized 1967-69 (Albany only). In service in: USA (3) Albany, Columbus, Chicago. The twin towers amidships are most distinctive.

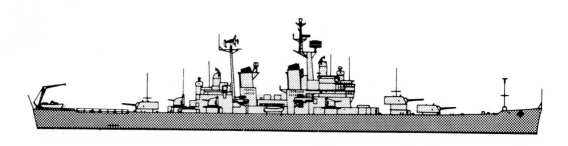

673	508	337	168	
205·2	154	103	51	FEET
				METRES 0

Displacement, tons: 13 600 standard, 17 200 full load
Dimensions, metres: 205·2 × 21·3 × 7·9 (673 × 69·9 × 25·9 ft)
Missiles: 2 twin Terrier aft (*Boston* and *Canberra*)
Guns: 9—8 in, 6—8 in (*Boston* and *Canberra*), 10 or 12—5 in dp, up to 20—3 in AA

Main machinery: 4 geared turbines (General Electric), 120 000 shp; 4 shafts
Speed, knots: 33
Complement: 1 969 (less in *Saint Paul, Quincy, Boston* and *Canberra*)
Building dates: 1941-46

NOTES: In service in: USA (9) Boston, Canberra, Quincy, Pittsburg, St Paul, Helena, Bremerton, Los Angeles, Toledo.   St Paul, Helena *and* Los Angeles *have improved flagship facilities, involving a pylon foretopmast in lieu of a pole.* Boston *and* Canberra *converted in 1951-52 to Terriers in place of after 8-in turret with addition· of extra radar.*

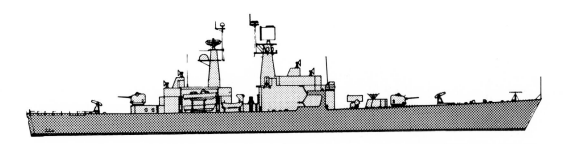

596	449	298	149	FEET
181·7	136	91	45	METRES 0

Displacement, tons: 10 150 full load
Dimensions, metres: 181·7 × 18·6 × 9 (596 × 61 × 29·5 ft)
Missiles: 2 single Tartar D surface-to-air launchers
Guns: 2—5 in dp (single)
A/S weapons: A/S torpedo launchers, 1 ASROC 8-tube launcher

Main machinery: 2 geared turbines; 2 shafts; 2 pressurized water-cooled D2G reactors
Speed, knots: 30
Complement: Approx 550
Building dates: 1970 onwards

NOTES: Due in service in: USA (2) California, South Carolina. *These large ships are classified as 'frigates' by the USN.*

TYPE: CRUISER (CLG) **CLASS: 'GALVESTON'** (converted 'Cleveland' class) USA

610	458	305	153	FEET
185·9	139	93	46	METRES 0

Displacement, tons: 10 670 standard, 14 600 full load
Dimensions, metres: 185·9 × 20·2 × 7·6 (610 × 66·3 × 25 ft)
Aircraft: Utility helicopter carried
Missiles: 1 twin Talos or Terrier surface-to-air launcher
Guns: 6—6 in, 6—5 in dp (*Galveston* and *Topeka*), 3—6 in, 2—5 in dp (remainder)

Main machinery: 4 geared turbines (General Electric), 10 000 shp; 4 shafts
Speed, knots: 31·6
Complement: 1 200-1 680
Building dates: 1942-45

NOTES: Conversion 1956-60. In service in: USA (6) Springfield, Little Rock, Oklahoma City, Providence, Galveston, Topeka. *The first four have additional flagship facilities, the first pair operating in the Mediterranean, the second in the Pacific, whilst the last two are in reserve.*

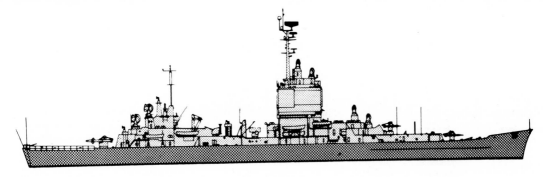

721·2	544	361	180	FEET
220	165	110	55	METRES 0

Displacement, tons: 14 200 standard, 17 350 full load
Dimensions, metres: 220 × 22·3 × 8·8 (721·2 × 73·2 × 29 ft)
Aircraft: Utility helicopter carried
Missiles: 1 twin Talos surface-to-air launcher, 2 twin Terrier surface-to-air launchers
Guns: 2—5 in dp (singles)
A/S weapons: 1 ASROC 8-tube launcher, 2 triple torpedo launchers

Main machinery: 2 geared turbines (General Electric) from 2 water-cooled C1W nuclear reactors; approx 80 000 shp; 2 shafts
Speed, knots: Approx 35
Complement: 1 000
Building dates: 1957-61

NOTES: *Is the first nuclear-powered surface warship and the first warship to have a guided missile main battery. In service in: USA (1). The box-shaped bridge is unique.*

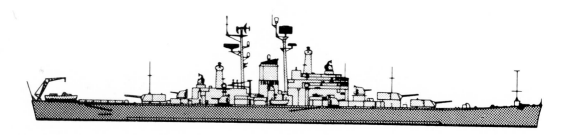

716·5	537	358	179	FEET
218·4	164	109	55	METRES 0

Displacement, tons: 17 000 standard, 21 500 full load
Dimensions, metres: 218·4 × 23·3 × 7·9 (716·5 × 76·3 × 26 ft)
Guns: 9—8 in, 12—5 in dual purpose, 4 or 20—3 in AA
Main machinery: 4 geared turbines (General Electric), 120 000 shp; 4 shafts

Speed, knots: 33
Complement: Approx 1 200
Building dates: 1945-49

NOTES: *In service in: USA (3) Des Moines, Newport News, Salem.* Newport News *has been given improved flagship facilities which involve much additional top-hamper.*

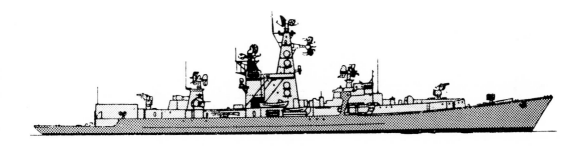

508·5 382 254 127 FEET 0
155 116 77 39 METRES

Displacement, tons: 5 140 standard, 6 500 full load
Dimensions, metres: 155 × 17 × 5·5 (508·5 × 55·8 × 18 ft)
Aircraft: 1 Hormone A helo
Missiles: 2 twin SSN 3B (Shaddock) launchers, 2 twin SAN 1 (Goa) launchers
Guns: 2 twin 57 mm
Torpedo tubes: 10—21 in in 2 mountings

A/S weapons: 2—12 barrelled launchers forward, 2—6 barrelled aft
Main machinery: Steam turbines; 4 boilers, 100 000 shp; 2 shafts
Speed, knots: 34
Complement: 400
Building dates: From 1964

NOTES: Currently in service in: USSR (4) Admiral Drozd, Admiral Zozulya, Vladivostok +1.

518·4	389	259	130	FEET
158	118	79	40	METRES 0

Displacement, tons: 6 000 standard, 7 500 full load
Dimensions, metres: 158 × 17 × 6 (518·4 × 55·8 × 19·7 ft)
Aircraft: 1 Hormone A can be embarked
Missiles: 2 quad SSN 10 launchers (25-mile missiles), 2 twin SAN 3 launchers
Guns: 2 twin 57 mm, 4 twin 30 mm

Torpedo tubes: 10—21 in in 2 mountings
A/S weapons: 2—12 barrelled launchers forward, 2—6 barrelled aft
Main machinery: Steam turbines, 4 boilers, 100 000 hp. 2 shafts
Speed, knots: 33
Complement: 500

NOTES: Currently in service in: USSR (2). Impressive ships whose performance has been improved over that of previous classes by the addition of Top-sail surveillance radar.

465·8	350	233	117	FEET	
142	106	71	35	METRES	0

Displacement, tons: 4 500 standard, 6 000 full load
Dimensions, metres: 142 × 15·8 × 5·3 (465·8 × 51·8 × 17·4 ft)
Aircraft: Helicopter pad aft
Missiles: 2 quad SSN 3B (Shaddock) launchers (1 forward, 1 aft), 1 twin SAN 1 (Goa) launcher
Guns: 2 twin 3 in

Torpedo tubes: 6—21 in in 2 mountings
A/S weapons: 2—12 barrelled launchers forward
Main machinery: 2 geared turbines; 4 boilers, 100 000 shp; 2 shafts
Speed, knots: 35
Complement: 390
Building dates: 1960-65

NOTES: Currently in service in: USSR (4) Admiral Fokin, Admiral Golovko, Grozny, Varyag.

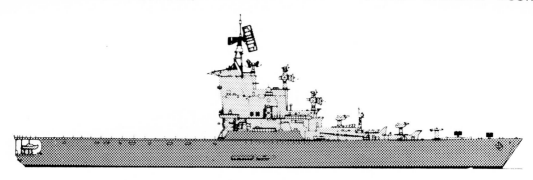

624·8	470	312	157	FEET
190·5	142	95	47	METRES 0

Displacement, tons: 15 000 standard
Dimensions, metres: 190·5 × 23 × 7·6 (624·8 × 75·9 × 24·9 ft)
Aircraft: 18 Hormone A helicopters
Missiles: 2 SAN 3
Guns: 4—57 mm (2 twin)
Torpedo tubes: 2 quin 21 in

A/S weapons: 1 missile launcher forward, 2—12 tube mortars
Main machinery: Geared turbines: 4 boilers, 100 000 shp; 2 shafts
Speed, knots: 30
Complement: 800
Special features: Flight deck 90 m × 35 m
Building dates: Completed 1967-69

NOTES: Currently in service in: USSR (2) Moskva, Leningrad. Ships with good sea-keeping qualities, extensive radar for all purposes and a comprehensive sonar outfit including VDS.

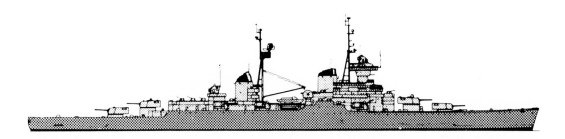

689	517	344	172	FEET	
210	157	105	52	METRES	0

Displacement tons: 15 450 standard
Dimensions, metres: 210 × 22 × 7·5 (689 × 72·2 × 24·5 ft)
Missiles: Twin SAN-2 aft in *Dzerzhinski* only
Guns: 4 triple 6 in, 6 twin 3·9 in, 22/32—37 mm (twins)
Torpedo tubes: 10—21 in
Mines: 140-250 can be carried

Main machinery: Geared turbines; 6 boilers, 130 000 shp; 2 shafts
Speed, knots: 34
Complement: Approx 1 000
Range: 8 700 at 18 knots
Building dates: 1950-60
Special features: Heavy armour belts from A turret to Y turret

NOTES: *Currently in service in: USSR* (12) Admiral Lazarev, Admiral Senjavin, Admiral Ushakov, Alexsandr Nevskii, Alexsandr Suvorov, Dmitri Pozharskiy, Dzerzhinski, Mikhail Kutusov, Murmansk, Oktyabrskaya Revolutsiya, Sverdlov, Zhdanov.

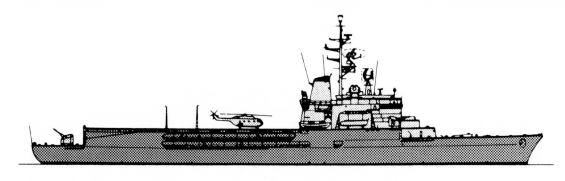

597·1	448	298	149	FEET
182	136	91	45	METRES 0

Displacement, tons: 10 000 standard, 12 365 full load
Dimensions, metres: 182 × 24 × 7·3 (597·1 × 78·7 × 24 ft)
Aircraft: 4-8 heavy A/S helicopters
Guns: 4—3·9 in (100 mm) single AA
Main machinery: Rateau-Bretagne geared turbines, 40 000 shp; 2 shafts

Speed, knots: 26·5 designed
Complement: 906
Range: 6 000 at 15 knots
Building dates: 1960-64

NOTES: In service in: France. A ship with a wartime role of commando support but used as a training ship in peace-time (190 cadets).

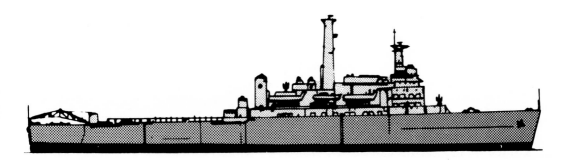

520	390	260	130	FEET	
158·5	119	79	40	METRES	0

Displacement, tons: 11 060 standard, 12 120 full load
Dimensions, metres: 158·5 × 24·4 × 6·2 (520 × 80 × 20·5 ft)
Aircraft: Flight deck facilities for 5 Wessex helicopters
Missiles, AA: 4 Seacat systems

Guns: 2—40 mm Bofors AA
Main machinery: 2 EE turbines, 22 000 shp; 2 shafts
Speed, knots: 21
Complement: 556 plus 111 troops
Building dates: 1962-67

NOTES: In service in: UK (2) Fearless, Intrepid. Designed for commando support, with a dock below the flight deck. They can use their 4 LCM(9) and 4 LCVP for ferrying tanks, lorries and men ashore.

TYPE: ASSAULT SHIP (LSD)   **CLASS: 'ANCHORAGE' USA**

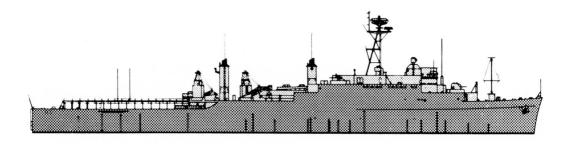

553·3	416	277	139	FEET
169	127	84	42	METRES 0

Displacement, tons: 13 650 full load
Dimensions, metres: 169 × 25·6 × 5·7 (553·3 × 84
  × 18·6 ft)
Aircraft: Helicopter platform fitted
Guns: 8—3 in AA (twin)

Main machinery: 2 geared turbines; 2 shafts
Speed, knots: 20+
Complement: 400
Building dates: 1967-72

NOTES: In service in: USA (5) Anchorage, Portland, Pensacola, Mount Vernon, Fort Fisher.

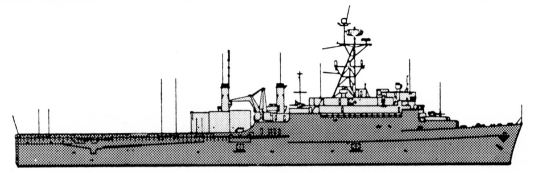

570	427	284	142	FEET
173·8	130	87	45	METRES 0

Displacement, tons: 10 000 light, 16 900 full load
Dimensions, metres: 173·8 × 25·6 × 7 (570 × 84 × 23 ft)
Aircraft: 6 UH-34 or CH-46 helicopters
Guns: 8—3 in (76 mm) 50 cal AA (twin)

Main machinery: 2 steam turbines, 24 000 shp; 2 shafts
Speed, knots: 20
Complement: 490
Building dates: 1963-71

NOTES: *In service in: USA (*12*)* Austin, Ogden, Duluth, Cleveland, Dubuque, Denver, Juneau, Coronado, Shreveport, Nashville, Trenton, Ponce. *Similar function to 'Fearless' class (UK). Larger than earlier 'Raleigh' class.*

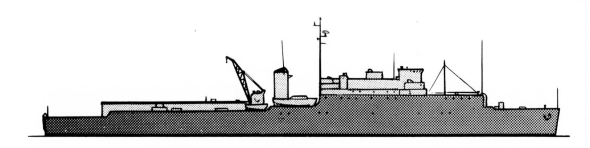

475·4	356	237	119	FEET
144·8	109	72	36	METRES 0

Displacement, tons: 4 790 standard, 9 375 full load
Dimensions, metres: 144·8 × 23·1 × 5·5 (475·4 × 76·2 × 18 ft)
Guns: 8 or 12—40 mm AA (2 quad plus 2 twin in some ships)

Main machinery: Geared turbines, 7 000 shp; 2 shafts
Speed, knots: 15·4
Complement: 265
Building dates: Completed 1946

NOTES: In service in: USA (11) Casa Grande, Rushmore, Shadwell, Cabildo, Catamount, Colonial, Comstock, Donner, Fort Marion, Tortuga, Whetstone; *Greece (1)* Nafkratoussa; *Spain (1)* Galicia.

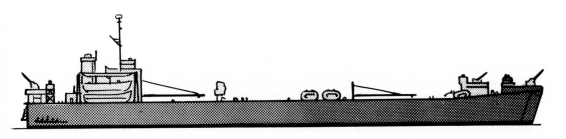

328	247	164	82	FEET
100	75	50	24	METRES 0

Displacement, tons: 1 653 standard, 4 080 full load
Dimensions, metres: 100 × 15·2 × 4·2 (328 × 50 × 14 ft)
Guns: 6—40 mm AA (2 twin, 2 single), reduced in some ships

Main machinery: GM diesels, 1 700 bhp; 2 shafts
Speed, knots: 11·6
Complement: 119
Building dates: Completed 1945

NOTES: In service in: USA (18), Brazil (1), China (16), Greece (5), Indonesia (8), Japan (3), South Korea (8), Malaysia (1), Mexico (1), Spain (1), Taiwan (21), Philippines (6), Singapore (1), Thailand (4), South Vietnam (6). The smallest of the 3 older classes of LST in the USN.

TYPE: ASSAULT SHIP (LSM)　　**CLASS: 'LSM' GREECE and others (USA)**

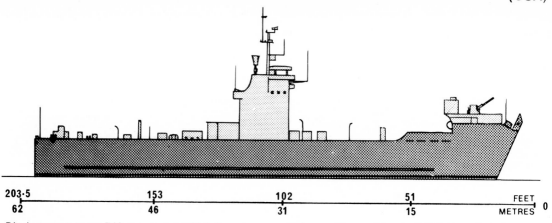

203·5	153	102	51	FEET
62	46	31	15	METRES　0

Displacement, tons: 743 standard, 1 000 full load
Dimensions, metres: 62 × 10·4 × 2·5 (203·5 × 34·2
　× 8·3 ft)
Guns: 2—40 mm

Main machinery: Diesels, 2 800 bhp; 2 shafts
Speed, knots: 12
Complement: 60
Building dates: 1945

NOTES: In service in: Greece (6), West Germany (2), Japan (1), Taiwan (4), Philippines (3), Thailand (3), Dominica (1). Included as a typical A/W ship although now out of date.

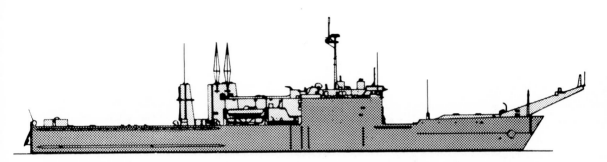

| 522·3 | 391 | 260 | 130 | FEET | 0 |
| 159·2 | 119 | 79 | 40 | METRES | |

Displacement, tons: 8 342 full load
Dimensions, metres: 159·2 × 21·2 × 4·5 (522·3 × 69·5 × 15 ft)
Guns: 4—3 in (twin)

Main machinery: 6 diesels (Alco), 16 000 hp; 2 shafts
Speed, knots: 20
Complement: 213 plus 379 troops
Building dates: 1966-72

NOTES: A fascinating new design.   In service in: USA (20).   See Index for names.

TYPE: ASSAULT SHIP (LSD)

CLASS: 'THOMASTON' USA

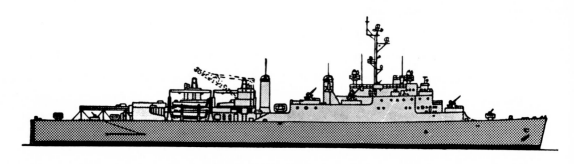

510	382	255	127	FEET
155·5	117	78	39	METRES 0

Displacement, tons: 6 880 light, 11 270 full load
Dimensions, metres: 155·5 × 25·6 × 5·7 (510 × 84 × 19 ft)
Aircraft: Helicopter platform fitted
Guns: 12—3 in 50 cal AA (twin)

Main machinery: Steam turbines, 23 000 shp; 2 shafts
Speed, knots: 24
Complement: 305 + 100 troops
Building dates: Completed 1957

NOTES: In service in: USA (8) Thomaston, Plymouth Rock, Fort Snelling, Point Defiance, Alamo, Spiegel Grove, Hermitage, Monticello.

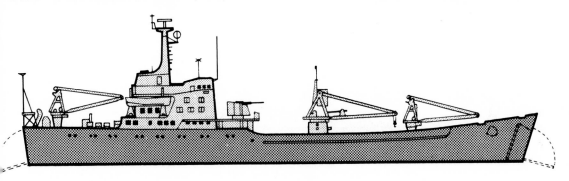

365·1	276	183	92	FEET
111·3	84	56	28	METRES 0

Displacement, tons: 4 100 standard, 5 800 full load
Dimensions, metres: 111·3 × 15·5 × 3·6 (365·1 × 51·2 × 12·1 ft)
Guns: 2—57 mm AA

Main machinery: Diesels, 8 000 bhp
Speed, knots: 15
Building dates: 1965 onwards

NOTES: In service in: USSR (8).

TYPE: AMPHIBIOUS SHIP (LCT)   **CLASS: 'POLNOCNY' USSR and others**

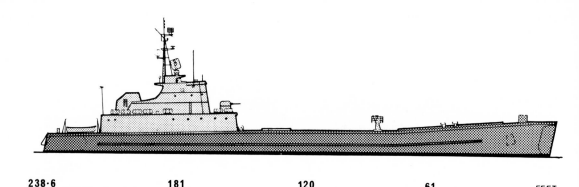

238·6   181   120   61   FEET
72·3   54   36   18   METRES   0

Displacement, tons: 780 standard, 1 000 full load
Dimensions, metres: 72·3 × 8·4 × 2·9 (238·6 × 27·7
  × 9·8 ft)
Armament: 2—14 barrelled rocket projectors

Main machinery: 2 diesels, 5 000 bhp
Speed, knots: 18
Building dates: 1961 onwards

NOTES: In service in: USSR (50), Poland (20), India (4—2 Type II). Carry at least 10 tanks. Type II has twin 30-mm turret forward of the bridge.

TYPE: DESTROYER

389·9	292	195	97	FEET	0
118·9	89	59	30	METRES	

Displacement, tons: 2 800 standard, 3 600 full load
Dimensions, metres: 118·9 × 13·1 × 5·5 (389·9 × 43 × 18 ft)
Guns: 6—4·5 in in 3 twin turrets, 2 forward and 1 aft; 6—40 mm or 2—40 mm
A/S weapons: Limbo in *Vampire* and *Vendetta*, Squid in remainder

Main machinery: English Electric geared turbines, 54 000 shp; 2 shafts
Speed, knots: 34·5 designed
Complement: 300-320
Range: 3 700 at 20 knots
Building dates: 1946-59

NOTES: *In service in: Australia (3)* Vampire, Vendetta, Duchess; *Peru (2)* Ferré, Palacios. *The modernization of the first two is considerably altering their silhouette—large fore-funnel, new masts, new after superstructure.*

424	318	212	106	FEET
129·2	97	65	33	METRES 0

Displacement, tons: 3 300 standard, 3 900 full load
Dimensions, metres: 129·2 × 13·4 × 5·5 (424 × 44 × 18 ft)
Aircraft: 1 WG 13 A/S helicopter
Missile launchers: Ikara A/S or Exocet surface-to-surface
Guns: 2—40 mm L/70, 1 or 2—4·5 in Mk 8
Torpedo tubes: 2 triple Mk 32

A/S weapons: 1 Bofors 375 mm twin tube A/S rocket launcher
Main machinery: CODOG system, 2 Rolls-Royce gas turbines = 30 knots, 4 MAN diesels = 22 knots
Complement: 200
Range: 5 300 miles at 17 knots
Building dates: 1972 on

NOTES: Under construction for Brazil (6),4 by Vosper Thornycroft and 2 in Brazil Constituição, Defensora, Inde-pendencia, Liberal, Niteroi, Uniao.

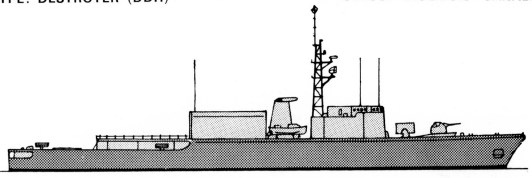

426	319	213	106	FEET
129·8	98	65	33	METRES 0

Displacement, tons: 4 050 full load
Dimensions, metres: 129·8 × 15·2 × 4·3 (426 × 50 × 14 ft)
Aircraft: 2 Sea King CHSS-2 A/S helicopters
Missiles: Sea Sparrow AA missiles will be fitted
Guns: 1 A/S mortar Mk 10; 1—5 in single dp
Torpedo tubes: 2 triple for A/S homing torpedoes

Main machinery: Gas turbines; 2 Pratt & Whitney FT4, 44 000 shp, + 2 Pratt & Whitney FT 12, 6 200 shp, for cruising; 2 shafts
Speed, knots: 27 designed
Range: 9 000 at economical speed
Building dates: 1969-73

NOTES: In service in: Canada (4 in 1972-73) Iroquois, Athabaskan, Huron, Algonquin.

517·1	388	258	129	FEET
157·6	119	79	39	METRES 0

Displacement, tons: 5 090 standard, 6 090 full load
Dimensions, metres: 157·6 × 15·5 × 6·1 (517·1 × 50·9 × 20 ft)
Missile launchers: Malafon rocket/homing torpedo single launcher, twin Masurca surface-air
Guns: 2—100 mm, 2—30 mm, automatic single AA
Torpedo launchers: 4 for A/S homing torpedoes

Main machinery: Double reduction geared turbines, 72 500 shp; 2 shafts
Speed, knots: 34
Complement: 426
Range: 5 000 at 18 knots
Building dates: 1962-69

NOTES: In service in: France (2) Suffren, Duquesne.

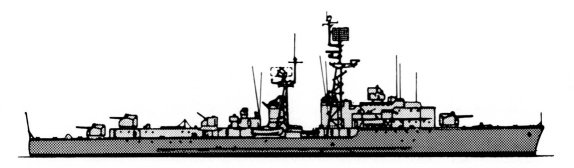

421·3	316	210	105	FEET	0
128·4	97	64	32	METRES	

Displacement, tons: 2 750 standard, 3 850 full load
Dimensions, metres: 128·4 × 13 × 5·6 (421·3 × 42·6 × 18·3 ft)
Missiles: Single Tartar Mk 13 AA in first four only
Guns: 6—5 in (twin mounts) except in first four, 4 or 6—57 mm, 6—20 mm
Torpedo tubes: 12—21·7 in (550 mm) in 4 triple mounts (6 ordinary, 6 ASM)

Main machinery: 2 Parsons geared turbines, 63 000 shp; 2 shafts
Speed, knots: 35 max
Complement: 293
Range: 5 000 at 18 knots
Building dates: 1951-57

NOTES: In service in: France (11) Bouvet, Du Chayla, Dupetit Thouars, Kersaint, Cassard, Chevalier Paul, Casabianca, D'Estrées, Guépratte, Mailié Brézé, Vauquelin.   Have been converted in three groups—the first four for SAM with loss of all their 5-in guns, the next two as leaders with loss of 2—57 mm and 6 tubes, whilst the last five were fitted for A/S with Malafon and Bofors launchers, VDS, new bow sonar and 2—3·9 in AA guns in lieu.

CLASS: 'T 53R (FORBIN)' FRANCE

422	317	211	105	FEET
128·6	97	64	32	METRES 0

Displacement, tons: 2 750 standard, 3 900 full load

Dimensions, metres: 128·6 × 12·7 × 5·4 (422 × 41·7 × 17·7 ft)

Guns: 6—5 in (3 twin), 6—2·25 in Bofors (3 twin), 2—20 mm

Torpedo tubes: 6—21·7 in (550 mm) ASM (2 triple) (also able to launch ordinary torpedoes)

A/S weapons: Sextuple Bofors *lance roquettes* howitzer

Main machinery: 2 ACL geared turbines, 63 000 shp; 2 shafts

Speed, knots: 32 sea, 34 max

Complement: 320

Range: 5 000 at 18 knots

Building dates: 1954-58

NOTES: In service in: France (5) Forbin, Jauréguiberry, La Bourdonnais, Tartu, Duperré. *First four act as air direction ships and the last is being converted to an ASW destroyer. In addition* La Galissonière *('T 56' class) has same hull as T 53s but with different armament and a helicopter hangar.*

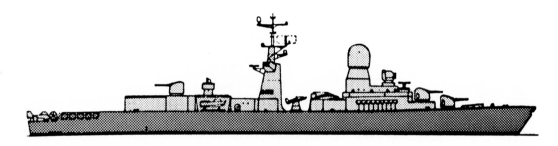

510·3	376	251	125	FEET
155·5	115	76	38	METRES 0

Displacement, tons: 4 580 standard, 5 745 full load
Dimensions, metres: 155·5 × 15·3 × ? (510·3 × 50·2 × ? ft)
Aircraft: 2 WG 13 ON ASW helicopters
Missile launchers: 6MM38 (Exocet) surface
Guns: 3—3·9 in AA
Torpedo tubes: Auto guided

A/S weapons: Malafon rocket /homing torpedo
Main machinery: Geared turbines, 54 400 shp; 2 shafts
Speed, knots: 31
Complement: 303
Range: 5 000 at 18 knots
Building dates: 1970 onwards

NOTES: Developed from the 'Aconit' design. In service in: France 1975 (2) Tourville, Duguay-Trouin.

CLASS: 'HAMBURG' WEST GERMANY

440·8	330	220	110	FEET
134	100	67	34	METRES 0

Displacement, tons: 3 340 standard, 4 330 full load
Dimensions, metres: 134 × 13·4 × 5·2 (440·8 × 44 × 17 ft)
Guns: 4—3·9 in single dp, 8—40 mm (4 twin) AA
Torpedo tubes: 5—21 in (533 mm), 3 bow and 2 stern, 2—12 in for A/S torpedoes

A/S weapons: 2 Bofors 4-barrelled DC mortars
Main machinery: 2 Wahodag dr geared turbines. 68 000 shp; 2 shafts
Speed, knots: 35·8 max, 18 economical
Complement: 280
Building dates: 1959-68

NOTES: In service in: West Germany (*4*) Bayern, Hamburg, Hessen, Schleswig-Holstein.

429·5	322	215	108	FEET
130·9	98	65	33	METRES

Displacement, tons: 3 201 standard, 3 941 full load
Dimensions, metres: 130·9 × 13·6 × 4·5 (429·5 × 44·7 × 14·8 ft)
Aircraft: 1 A/S light helicopter
Missiles, AA: 1 Tartar launcher aft
Guns: 2—5 in AA forward, 4—3 in
Torpedo tubes: 2 triple for A/S torpedoes

Main machinery: 2 double reduction geared turbines, 70 000 shp; 2 shafts
Speed, knots: 34 designed
Complement: 344
Range: 6 600 at 20 knots
Building dates: 1957-64

NOTES: In service in: Italy (2) Impavido, Intrepido. *Two new ships of an improved 'Impavido' class* (Ardito, Audace), *slightly larger but with the same armament, and an extra helicopter, will join the fleet in 1973.*

418·7	313	209	104	FEET
127·5	96	64	32	METRES 0

Displacement, tons: 2 755 standard, 3 800 full load
Dimensions, metres: 127·5 × 13·3 × 5·3 (418·7 × 43·5 × 17·5 ft)
Guns: 4—5 in, 16—40 mm
Torpedo tubes: 6 (2 triple) for A/S torpedoes
A/S weapons: 1 three-barrelled mortar, 4 DCT, 1 DC rack

Main machinery: 2 double reduction geared turbines, 65 000 shp; 2 shafts
Speed, knots: 34
Complement: 393
Range: 3 400 at 20 knots
Building dates: 1952-58

NOTES: In service in: Italy (2) Impetuoso, Indomito.

TYPE: DESTROYER

374		280		187		93		FEET	
114		85		57		28		METRES	0

Displacement, tons: 2 050
Dimensions, metres: 114 × 11·8 × 3·9 (374 × 38·7 × 12·8 ft)
Guns: 4—3 in (twin) AA
Torpedo launchers: 2 triple for A/S homing torpedoes
A/S weapons: Octuple ASROC or DASH installation (3 ships), 1 four-barrelled rocket launcher

Main machinery: 6 Mitsui or Mitsubishi B & W diesels, 26 500 bhp; 2 shafts
Speed, knots: 27-28
Complement: 210
Building dates: 1964-72

NOTES: In service in: Japan (10) Asagumo, Makigumo, Minegumo, Murakumo, Natsugumo, Yamagumo, Aokumo +3 building.

387·2	291	194	97	FEET
118	89	59	30	METRES 0

Displacement, tons: 2 350 standard, 2 890 full load
Dimensions, metres: 118 × 12 × 4 (387·2 × 39· 4 × 13·1 ft)
Guns: 3—5 in single dp, 4—3 in twin AA
Torpedo tubes: 4—21 in (533 mm) quad
A/S weapons: 1 US Mk 108 rocket launcher, 2 hedgehogs, 2 Y mortars, 2 DCT

Main machinery: 2 geared turbines, 45 000 shp; 2 shafts
Speed, knots: 32
Complement: 330
Building dates: 1958-60

NOTES: *In service in: Japan* (2) Akizuki, Teruzuki.

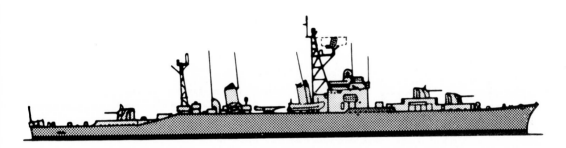

357·6	268	179	89	FEET
109	82	54	27	METRES 0

Displacement, tons: 1 700 standard, 2 500 full load
Dimensions, metres: 109 × 10·7 × 3·7 (357·6 × 35·1 × 12 ft)
Guns: 6—3 in (3 twin)
Torpedo tubes: 4—21 in (533 mm) quad
Torpedo launchers: 4 fixed, for A/S homing torpedoes
A/S weapons: 2 US model Mk 15 Hedgehogs, 2 Y guns, 2 DC racks

Main machinery: 2 Mitsubishi Escher-Weiss geared turbines, 35 000 shp; 2 shafts
Speed, knots: 32
Complement: 230
Building dates: 1956-60

NOTES: In service in: Japan (7) Ayanami, Isonami, Makinami, Onami, Shikinami, Takanami, Uranami.

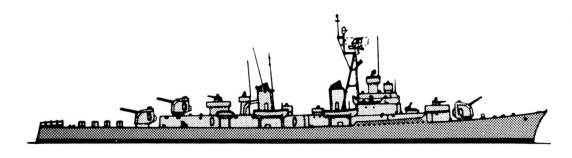

358·5	269	179	90	FEET
109·3	82	55	27	METRES 0

Displacement, tons: 1 700 standard, 2 340 full load
Dimensions, metres: 109·3 × 10·5 × 3·7 (358·5 × 34·5 × 12 ft)
Guns: 3—5 in dp, 8—40 mm (2 quad) AA
Torpedo tubes: For short, homing torpedoes
A/S weapons: 2 Hedgehogs, 1 DC rack, 4 K guns

Main machinery: 2 sets geared turbines, 30 000 shp; 2 shafts
Speed, knots: 30
Complement: 240
Range: 6 000 at 18 knots
Building dates: 1954-56

NOTES: In service in: Japan (2) Harukaze, Yukikaze.

380·5	285	190	95	FEET 0
116	87	58	29	METRES

Displacement, tons: 2 497 standard, 3 070 full load
Dimensions, metres: 116 × 11·7 × 5·2 (380·5 × 38·5 × 17 ft)
Guns: 4—4·7 in (twin turrets), 4—40 mm
A/S weapons: 2 four-barrelled depth charge mortars (Limbo type)

Main machinery: 2 Werkspoor geared turbines, 60 000 shp; 2 shafts
Speed, knots: 36
Complement: 284
Building dates: 1951-58

NOTES: In service in: Netherlands (8) Friesland, Groningen, Limburg, Overijssel, Drenthe, Utrecht, Rotterdam, Amsterdam.

CLASS: 'HOLLAND' NETHERLANDS

371·1	278	185	93	FEET
113·1	85	56	28	METRES 0

Displacement, tons: 2 215 standard, 2 765 full load
Dimensions, metres: 113·1 × 11·4 × 5·1 (371·1 × 37·5
    × 16·8 ft)
Guns: 4—4·7 in, 1—40 mm
A/S weapons: 2 4-barrelled DC mortars

Main machinery: Werkspoor Parsons geared turbines,
    45 000 shp; 2 shafts
Speed, knots: 32
Complement: 247
Building dates: 1950-55

NOTES: In service in: Netherlands (4) Holland, Zeeland, Noord Brabant, Gelderland.

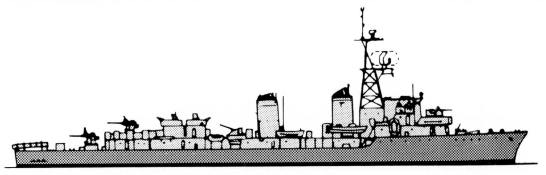

308·2	231	154	77	FEET
94	70	47	23	METRES 0

Displacement, tons: 1 227 standard, 1 550 full load
Dimensions, metres: 94 × 9·3 × 5·2 (308·2 × 30·5 × 17·1 ft)
Guns: 2—3 in dp, 2—40 mm AA
Torpedo racks: 2 side launching for A/S torpedoes (6 torpedoes)
A/S weapons: 2 Hedgehogs, 8 mortars, 2 DC racks

Main machinery: Rateau-Bretagne geared turbines, 28 000 shp; 2 shafts
Speed, knots: 31·6
Complement: 191
Range: 6 400 at 14 knots
Building dates: 1945-65

NOTES: In service in: Spain (8) Audaz, Furor, Intrépido, Meteoro, Osado, Rayo, Relãmpago, Temerario. All laid down at Ferrol in 1945. Last two not launched until 1960-61—as a result completion spread from 1953 to 1965. All modernized in early 1960s.

TYPE: DESTROYER   **CLASS: MODIFIED 'OQUENDO' SPAIN**

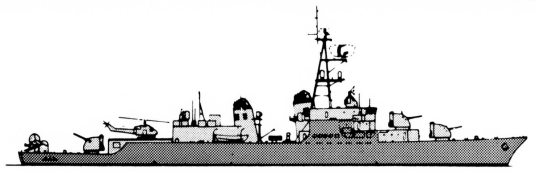

391·5	294	196	98	FEET
119·3	90	60	30	METRES 0

Displacement, tons: 3 000 standard, 3 587 full load
Dimensions, metres: 119·3 × 13 × 5·6 (391·5 × 42·7 × 18·4 ft)
Aircraft: 1 A/S helicopter
Guns: 6—5 in
Torpedo tubes: 2 triple launchers for A/S torpedoes, 2—21 in fixed tubes

Main machinery: 2 Rateau-Bretagne geared turbines, 60 000 shp; 2 shafts
Speed, knots: 31
Complement: 296
Range: 4 500 at 15 knots
Building dates: 1951-70

NOTES: In service in: Spain (2) Marqués de la Ensenada, Roger de Lauria. *A modification of the 'Oquendo' which, though slightly smaller, has very roughly the same silhouette with one less turret forward.*

397·2	298	198	99	FEET	
121	91	60	30	METRES	0

Displacement, tons: 2 800 standard, 3 400 full load
Dimensions, metres: 121 × 12·6 × 4·5 (397·2 × 41·3
   × 14·8 ft)
Missiles, surface: 1 rocket launcher RB08
Guns: 4—4·7 in (120 mm) dual purpose, 2—57 mm,
   6—40 mm AA
Torpedo tubes: 8—21 in (quads)

Mines: Can be fitted for minelaying
Main machinery: De Laval double reduction geared
   turbines, 58 000 shp; 2 shafts
Speed, knots: 35
Complement: 290
Range: 6 000 at 20 knots
Building dates: 1951-56

NOTES: In service in: Sweden (2) Halland, Småland.

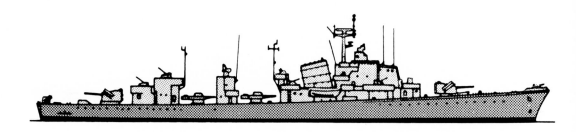

367·5	276	184	92	FEET
112	84	56	28	METRES 0

Displacement, tons: 2 000 standard, 2 400 full load
Dimensions, metres: 112 × 11·2 × 3·4 (367·5 × 36·8
   × 11·2 ft)
Guns: 4—4·7 in (120 mm) dp, 6—40 mm AA
Torpedo tubes: 6—21 in (533 mm) (2 triple)
A/S weapons: 1 triple-barrelled depth charge mortar
Mines: 60 can be carried

Main machinery: De Laval geared turbines, 44 000 shp:
   2 shafts
Speed, knots: 35
Complement: 210·
Range: 2 500 at 20 knots
Building dates: 1943-49

NOTES: Modernized 1960-63. In service in: Sweden (2) Öland, Uppland.

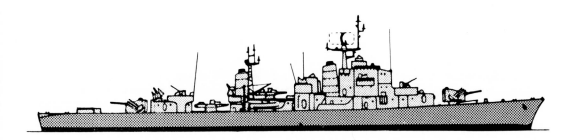

367·5	276	184	92	FEET
112	84	56	28	METRES

0

Displacement, tons,: 2 100 standard, 2 600 full load
Dimensions, metres: 112 × 11·2 × 3·7 (367·5 × 36·8 × 12 ft)
Missile launchers: 1 quadruple Seacat surface-to-air
Guns: 4– 4·7 in (120 mm), 4 to 7—40 mm AA
Torpedo tubes: 6—21 in (2 triple)
A/S weapons: Triple-barrelled DC mortar

Mines: 60 can be carried
Main machinery: De Laval turbines, 40 000 shp; 2 shafts
Speed, knots: 35
Complement: 244
Range: 4 400 at 20 knots
Building dates: 1955-59

NOTES: In service in: Sweden (4) Gästrikland, Hälsingland, Östergötland, Södermanland.

CLASS: 'SHEFFIELD' (Type 42) UK
ARGENTINA

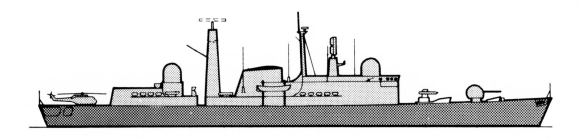

410	307	205	102	FEET
125	94	62	31	METRES 0

Displacement, tons: 3 500 approx full load
Dimensions, metres: 125 × 14·3 × 6·7 (410 × 47 × 22 ft)
Aircraft: 1 twin-engined Lynx A/S helicopter
Missile launchers: 1 twin Sea Dart medium range surface-to-air (surface-to-surface capability)
Guns: 1—4·5 in automatic, 2—20 mm Oerlikon

A/S weapons: Helicopter launched torpedoes
Main machinery: Rolls-Royce Olympus + Tyne gas turbines, 50 000 shp; 2 shafts
Speed, knots: 30 approx
Complement: 280
Range: 4 000 + at 18 knots
Building dates: 1970 on

NOTES: *Still under construction for UK (6) Sheffield, Birmingham, Coventry + 3; Argentina (2).*

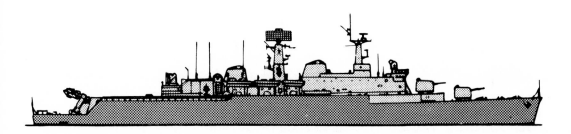

520·5	390	260	130	FEET
158·7	119	79	40	METRES 0

Displacement, tons: 5 440 standard, 6 200 full load
Dimensions, metres: 158·7 × 16·5 × 6·1 (520·5 × 54 × 20 ft)
Aircraft: 1 Wessex helicopter
Missile launchers: 1 twin Seaslug aft, 2 quad Seacat abaft after funnel
Guns: 4—4·5 in, 2 twin turrets forward, 2—20 mm single

Main machinery: 2 sets geared steam turbines, 30 000 shp; 4 gas turbines, 30 000 shp; 2 shafts. Total 60 000 shp
Speed, knots: 32·5 max
Complement: 471
Building dates: 1959-70

NOTES: In service in: UK (8) Devonshire, Hampshire, Kent, London, Fife, Glamorgan, Norfolk, Antrim. Of a similar size is the single ship of the Type 82, Bristol, which, with Sea Dart missiles, has a lower quarter-deck, different radar and only 1—4·5 in gun.

TYPE: DESTROYER   **CLASS: 'ALLEN M SUMNER' and modernizations USA and others**

376·5	283	188	94	FEET
114·8	86	57	29	METRES 0

Displacement, tons: 2 200 standard, 3 320 full load
Dimensions, metres: 114·8 × 12·4 × 5·8 (376·5 × 40·9 × 19 ft)
Guns: 6—5 in dual purpose (twin); 4—3 in AA (twin) (removed in modernizations)
A/S weapons: 2 fixed Hedgehogs, depth charges, 2 triple torpedo launchers (Mk 32)

Main machinery: 2 geared turbines, 60 000 shp; 2 shafts
Speed, knots: 34
Complement: 274
Building dates: 1944-46

NOTES: In service in: USA (5 plus 24 Fram II), Argentina (2), Greece (2), Spain (1), Turkey (1), Italy (1), Venezuela (1), Colombia (1), Iran (2), Taiwan (6). See Index for names. The 24 USN Fram II conversions have much heavier top-hamper and radar aerials with a helicopter pad abaft the mainmast.

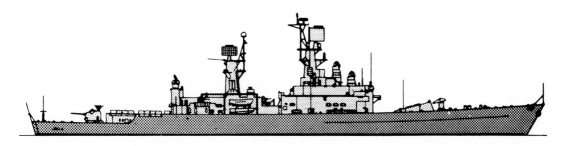

547	410	273	136	FEET
166·7	125	83	42	METRES 0

Displacement, tons: 6 570 standard, 7 930 full load
Dimensions, metres: 166·7 × 16·7 × 8·7 (547 × 54·8 × 28 ft)
Aircraft: Facilities for helicopters
Missiles: 1 twin Terrier/ASROC launcher
Guns: 1—5 in dp, 2—3 in AA (single)
A/S weapons: ASROC, 2 triple torpedo launchers, Mk 32

Main machinery: 2 geared turbines (GEC or De Laval), 85 000 shp; 2 shafts
Speed, knots: 34
Complement: 418
Building dates: 1962-67

NOTES: In service in: USA (9) Belknap, Josephus Daniels, Wainwright, Jouett, Horne, Sterett, Fox, William H Standley, Biddle. *The Mk 10 missile launcher up forward can discharge either Terrier AA missiles or ASROC ASW missiles. Classified as 'frigates' in USN.*

CLASS: 'CHARLES F ADAMS' USA
and others

437	327	218	109	FEET	0
132·8	92	61	31	METRES	

Displacement, tons: 3 370 standard, 4 500 full load
Dimensions, metres: 132·8 × 14·3 × 6·1 (437 × 47 × 20 ft)
Missiles: 1 single or twin Tartar surface-to-air launcher
Guns: 2—5 in dual purpose
A/S weapons: 1 ASROC 8-tube launcher, 2 triple torpedo launchers (Mk 32)

Main machinery: 2 geared steam turbines (General Electric or Westinghouse), 70 000 shp; 2 shafts
Speed, knots: 35
Complement: 354
Building dates: 1958-64

NOTES: In service in: USA (23), Australia (3), West Germany (3). See Index for names.

512·5	384	256	128	FEET
156·2	117	78	39	METRES 0

Displacement, tons: 4 700 standard, 5 800 full load
Dimensions, metres: 156·2 × 15·9 × 7·6 (512·5 × 52·5 × 25 ft)
Missiles: 1 twin Terrier surface-to-air launcher
Guns: 1—5 in dp, 4—3 in AA twin (removed during modernization)
A/S weapons: 1 ASROC 8-tube launcher, 2 triple torpedo launchers (Mk 32)

Main machinery: 2 geared turbines, 85 000 shp; 2 shafts
Speed, knots: 34
Complement: 370
Building dates: 1957-61

NOTES: In service in: USA (10) Coontz, Farragut, Preble, Dewey, Luce, Macdonough, King, Mahan, Dahlgren, William V Pratt. First five have been modernized, remainder are planned to be. Classified as 'frigates' in USN.

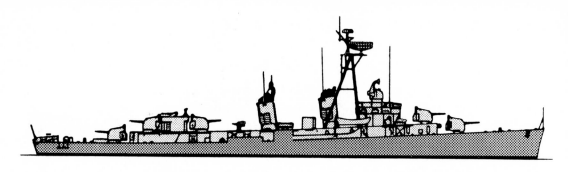

376·5	283	188	94	FEET
114·8	86	57	29	METRES 0

Displacement, tons: 2 100 standard, 3 050 full load
Dimensions, metres: 114·8 × 12 × 5·5 (376·5 × 39·5 × 18 ft)
Guns: 4 or 5—5 in, 6—3 in or 6—40 mm
Torpedo tubes: 5 or 10—21 in (quintuple)
A/S weapons: 2 fixed Hedgehogs, 1 DC rack; 2 torpedo launchers

Main machinery: 2 sets geared turbines, 60 000 shp; 2 shafts
Speed, knots: 35
Complement: 250
Range: 6 000 at 15 knots
Building dates: 1942-43

NOTES: In service in: USA (31), Argentina (5), Brazil (6), Taiwan (2), Chile (2), Colombia (1), West Germany (4), Greece (6), Japan (2), Italy (2), South Korea (3), Mexico (2), Peru (2), Spain (5), Turkey (5). In addition there are 21 later Fletcher class in the USN, similar to the original. See Index for names.

418·4	313	209	104	FEET
127·4	96	64	32	METRES 0

Displacement, tons: 2 800 standard, 4 000 full load
Dimensions, metres: 127·4 × 13·7 × 6·1 (418·4 × 45·2 × 20 ft)
Missiles: 1 single Tartar (in DLG mod)
Guns: 1, 2 or 3—5 in dual purpose, 2 or 4—3 in AA (twin)
A/S weapons: 2 triple torpedo launchers (Mk 32), 2 Hedgehogs or 1 ASROC 8-tube launcher

Main machinery: 2 geared turbines (General Electric or Westinghouse), 70 000 shp; 2 shafts
Speed, knots: 33
Complement: 292 in unmodified ships, 335-340 in others
Building dates: 1953-59

NOTES: In service in: USA(18) Forrest Sherman, Bigelow, Mullinnix, Hull, Richard S Edwards, Turner Joy (all un-modified), Barry, Davis, Jonas Ingram, Manley, Du Pont, Blandy, Edson, Morton (ASW conversion with ASROC aft). Decatur, John Paul Jones, Parsons, Somers (DLG conversion with Tartar and 1—5 inch).

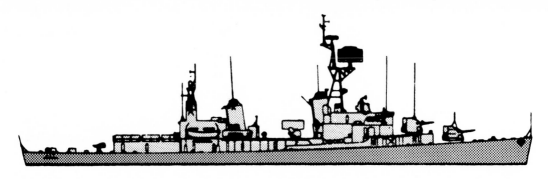

| 390·5 | 292 | 195 | 97 | FEET | 0 |
| 119 | 89 | 59 | 30 | METRES | |

Displacement, tons: 2 425 standard, 3 500 full load
Dimensions, metres: 119 × 12·4 × 5·8 (390·5 × 40·9 × 19 ft)
Guns: 4—5 in dp (twin)
A/S weapons: 1 ASROC 8-tube launcher, 2 triple torpedo launchers (Mk 32); facilities for small helicopter

Main machinery: 2 geared turbines (General Electric or Westinghouse), 60 000 shp; 2 shafts
Speed, knots: 34
Complement: 274
Range: 5 800 at 15 knots
Building dates: 1944-49, conversion 1959-64

NOTES: In service in: USA (71), Turkey (2) Adatepe, Kocatepe; Spain (2), Greece (1). Eight of these ships have 2 twin 5-inch mounts forward, the remainder having them in A and Y positions. See Index for names.

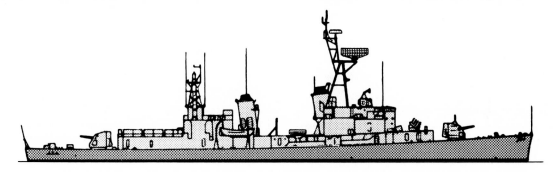

390·5	292	195	97	FEET	0
119	89	59	30	METRES	

Displacement, tons: 2 425 standard, 3 500 full load
Dimensions, metres: 119 × 12·4 × 5·8 (390·5 × 40·9 × 19 ft)
Aircraft: Facilities for small helicopter
Guns: 4—5 in dual purpose (twins in A and Y positions)
Torpedo tubes: 2 fixed (Mk 25)
A/S weapons: 1 large, trainable Hedgehog (Mk 15), 2 triple torpedo launchers (Mk 32)

Main machinery: 2 geared turbines, 60 000 shp; 2 shafts
Speed, knots: 34
Complement: 275
Building dates: 1945-47, conversion 1962

NOTES: In service in: USA (8) Norris, McCaffery (unconverted), Chevalier, Benner, Perkins (ex-radar pickets), Kenneth D Bailey, Goodrich, Duncan (radar pickets); Greece (1) Themistocles; Taiwan (1) Fu Wang.

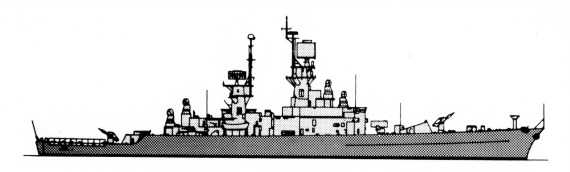

533	399	266	133	FEET
162·5	122	81	41	METRES 0

Displacement, tons: 5 670 standard, 7 800 full load
Dimensions, metres: 162·5 × 16·6 × 7·4 (533 × 54·9 × 24·5 ft)
Missiles: 2 twin Terrier surface-to-air launchers
Guns: 4—3 in (twin) AA
A/S weapons: 1 ASROC 8-tube launcher, 2 triple torpedo launchers (Mk 32)

Main machinery: 2 geared turbines, 85 000 shp; 2 shafts
Speed, knots: 34
Complement: 396
Building dates: 1959-64

NOTES: In service in: USA (9) Leahy, Harry E Yarnell, Worden, Dale, Richmond K Turner, Gridley, England, Halsey, Reeves. All modernized (missiles and electronics) between 1967 and 1972. Classified as 'frigates' in USN.

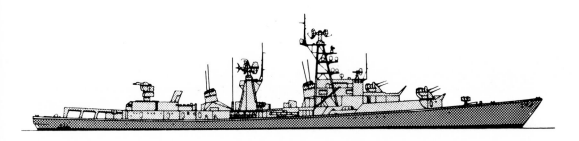

456	342	228	114	FEET
139	104	69	35	METRES 0

Displacement, tons: 3 700 standard, 4 600 full load
Dimensions, metres: 139 × 14·9 × 5 (456 × 48·9 × 16·4 ft)
Aircraft: Light pad aft
Missiles: 1 twin SAN 1 (Goa) aft
Guns: 2 quad 57 mm forward or 4 twin 30 mm
Torpedo tubes: 2—21 in quintuple mountings

A/S weapons: 3—12 barrelled launchers
Main machinery: 2 geared turbines, 4 boilers, 80 000 shp; 2 shafts
Speed, knots: 34
Complement: 350
Building dates: Converted from 1967
Special features: Converted from 'Krupny' class whilst building

NOTES: Currently in service in : USSR (4) Gremyashchyi +3.

470·9	353	235	118	FEET
143·3	106	71	36	METRES 0

Displacement, tons: 4 300 standard, 5 200 full load
Dimensions, metres: 143·3 × 15·9 × 5·8 (470·9 × 52·5 × 19 ft)
Missiles: 2 twin SAN 1 (Goa) forward and aft
Guns: 2 twin 3 in forward and aft
Torpedo tubes: 1 quintuple 21 in amidships

A/S weapons: 2 12-barrelled launchers forward, 2 6-barrelled aft
Main machinery: 8 sets gas turbines, 96 000 hp; 2 shafts
Speed, knots: 35
Building dates: From 1961

NOTES: Currently in service in: USSR (15) Obraztsovyi, Otlitnyi, Otnasnyi, Otvashnyi, Provedyonny, Provornyi, Slavny, Soobrazitelnyi, Steregushchyi, Stojkyi, Strogyi +4.

416·7	312	208	104	FEET	
127	95	63	32	METRES	0

Displacement, tons: 3 000 standard, 4 000 full load
Dimensions, metres: 127 × 12·9 × 4·9 (416·7 × 42·3 × 16·1 ft)
Missile launchers: 1 for SS-N-1 (Scrubber) missiles
Guns: 16—57 mm (4 quad) AA
A/S weapons: 2 16-barrelled rocket launchers on forecastle

Main machinery: Geared turbines, 72 000 shp; 2 shafts
Speed, knots: 36 max
Complement: 350
Rebuilding dates: 1957-59

NOTES: In service in: USSR (4) Bedovyy, Neulovimyi +2. A redesign on 'Kotlin' class hulls with SSN-1 launcher aft in place of guns.

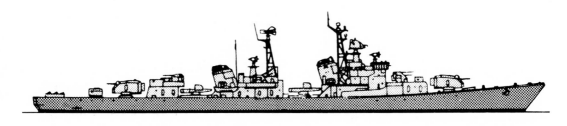

414·9	312	207	104	FEET
126·5	95	63	32	METRES 0

Displacement, tons: 2 850 standard, 3 885 full load
Dimensions, metres: 126·5 × 12·9 × 4·9 (414·9 × 42·3 × 16·1 ft)
Guns: 4—5·1 in (130 mm) (2 twin),16—45 mm AA
Torpedo tubes: 10—21 in (533 mm)
A/S weapons: 6 side thrown DC projectors or 2 16-barrelled ASW rocket launchers

Mines: 80 if required
Main machinery: Geared turbines, 72 000 shp; 2 shafts
Speed, knots: 36
Complement: 285
Building dates: 1954-57

NOTES: In service in: USSR (20).   See Index for names. The 'Tallin' class Neustrashimyi is not unlike the Kotlins, having the same hull.

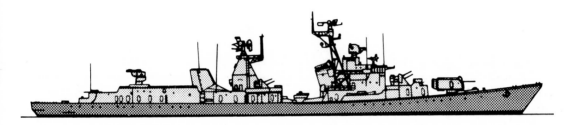

414·9	312	207	104	FEET	
126·5	95	63	32	METRES	0

Displacement, tons: 2 850 standard, 3 885 full load
Dimensions, metres: 126·5 × 12·9 × 4·9 (414·9 × 42·3 × 16·1 ft)
Missile launchers: 1 twin SAN-1 (Goa) mounted aft
Guns: 2—3·9 in (twin), 4—57 mm AA (quad)
A/S weapons: 6 side thrown DC projectors or 2 12-barrelled ASW rocket launchers

Main machinery: Geared turbines, 72 000 shp; 2 shafts
Speed, knots: 36
Complement: 285
Building dates: 1954-57 as Kotlin class

NOTES: In service in: USSR (7), Poland (1).   Converted from normal Kotlins between 1961and1969 with twin SAN-1 in place of the after turret.   After funnels differ.

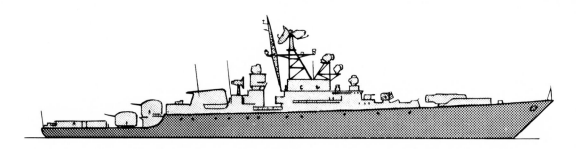

404·8	303	202	101	FEET	0
123·4	93	62	31	METRES	

Displacement, tons: 4 800 standard
Dimensions, metres: 123·4 × 14 × 5   (404·8 × 45·9 × 16·4 ft)
Missile launchers: 4 short range surface-to-surface and 2 twin SAN-4 surface-to-air missiles
Torpedo tubes: 8—21 in amidships (2 quads)

Guns: 4—3 in (2 twin), 4—30 mm (2 twin) AA
A/S weapons: 2 12-barrelled forward for rocket missiles
Main machinery: 8 sets of gas turbines, 112 000 shp; 2 shafts
Speed, knots: 38

NOTES: In service in: USSR (3).

452·8	340	226	113	FEET
138	103	69	34	METRES　0

Displacement, tons: 3 650 standard, 4 650 full load
Dimensions, metres: 138 × 14·6 × 5 (452·8 × 47·9 × 16·5 ft)
Missile launchers: 2 mountings, 1 forward, 1 aft, for SS-N-1 (Scrubber) missiles
Guns: 16—57 mm (4 quadruple) AA

Torpedo launchers: 6 (2 triple) for 21 in A/S torpedoes
Main machinery: Geared steam turbines, 80 000 shp; 2 shafts
Speed, knots: 34
Complement: 360
Building dates: 1958 on

NOTES: In service in: USSR (4).　See Index for names. Three of this class were converted to carry SAN-1 missiles only in 1967-68 and became the 'Kanin' class.

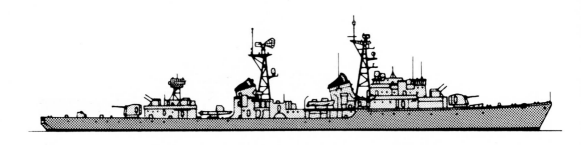

395·2	297	198	99	FEET
120·5	90	60	30	METRES 0

Displacement, tons: 2 600 standard, 3 500 full load
Dimensions, metres: 120·5 × 11·8 × 4·6 (395·2 × 38·9 × 15·1 ft)
Guns: 4—5·1 in (2 twin), 2—3·4 in (twin), 8—37 mm (4 twin)
Torpedo tubes: 10—21 in
A/S weapons: 4 DCT

Mines: 80 if required
Main machinery: Geared turbines, 60 000 shp; 2 shafts
Speed, knots: 33
Complement: 260
Range: 3 900 at 13 knots
Building dates: Approx 1954 on

NOTES: In service in: USSR (45), Egypt (4), Indonesia (4), Poland (2). See Index for names.

402   303   201   100   FEET 0
122·5   92   61   31   METRES

Displacement, tons: 2 600 standard, 3 670 full load
Dimensions, metres: 122·5 × 13·1 × 5·8 (402 × 43 × 19 ft)
Missiles: 2 quad Seacat in *Esparta*
Guns, AA: 6—4·5 in (3 twin), 16—40 mm (8 twin) or 4—40 mm (2 twin) (*Esparta*)
Torpedo tubes: 3—21 in (533 mm) triple except *Esparta*
A/S weapons: 2 DCT, 2 DC racks, and Squids

(except *Aragua*)
Main machinery: Parsons geared turbines, 50 000 2 shafts
Speed, knots: 34
Complement: 256
Range: 10 000 at 10 knots
Building dates: 1951-56

NOTES: *In service in: Venezuela* (3) Nueva Esparta, Zulia, Aragua. *Built by Vickers* (*Barrow*).

370	278	186	93	FEET
112·8	85	57	28	METRES 0

Displacement, tons: 2 100 standard, 2 700 full load
Dimensions, metres: 112·8 × 12·5 × 5·3 (370 × 41 × 17·3 ft)
Missile launchers: 1 quad for Seacat
Guns: 2—4·5 in dp
A/S weapons: 1 launcher for Ikara, 1 Limbo 3-barrelled mortar

Main machinery: 2 double reduction geared turbines, 30 000 shp; 2 shafts
Speed, knots: 30
Complement: 247-250
Building dates: 1956-71

NOTES: In service in: Australia (6) Derwent, Parramatta, Stuart, Yarra, Swan, Torrens. Modifications of RN Type 12; all built in Australia.

371		278		186		93		FEET	0
113·1		85		57		28		METRES	

Displacement, tons: 2 400 standard, 3 000 full load
Dimensions, metres: 113·1 × 12·8 × 4·4 (371 × 42 × 14·4 ft)
Aircraft: 1 CHSS-2 Sea King helicopter
Guns: 2—3 in (twin) AA

A/S weapons: 1 Mk 10 3-barrelled mortar in after well
Main machinery: Geared turbines, 30 000 shp; 2 shafts
Speed, knots: 28
Complement: 246
Building dates: 1960-64

NOTES: *In service in: Canada* (2) Nipigon, Annapolis.

CLASS: 'MACKENZIE' CANADA

366	275	183	90	FEET
111·5	84	56	27	METRES 0

Displacement, tons: 2 380 standard, 2 890 full load
Dimensions, metres: 111·5 × 12·8 × 4·1 (366 × 42 × 13·5 ft)
Guns: 4—3 in (2 twin) AA
A/S weapons: 2 Mk 10 mortars in well aft

Main machinery: Geared turbines, 30 000 shp; 2 shafts
Speed, knots: 28
Complement: 245
Building dates: 1958-63

NOTES: *In service in: Canada*(4)Mackenzie, Saskatchewan, Yukon, Qu'Appelle. *Classified as destroyer escorts (DDE) in RCN.*

| 367·4 | | 276 | | 184 | | 92 | | FEET | 0 |
| 112 | | 85 | | 57 | | 28 | | METRES | |

Displacement, tons: 2 370 standard, 2 880 full load
Dimensions, metres: 112 × 12·8 × 4·2 (367·4 × 42 × 14·1 ft)
Guns: 4—3 in (76 mm) (2 twin)
A/S weapons: 2 Mk 10 triple-barrelled mortar before conversion and ASROC and Mk 10 after conversion

Main machinery: Geared turbines, 30 000 shp; 2 shafts
Speed, knots: 28
Complement: 248-250
Building dates: 1953-59

NOTES: In service in: Canada (7) Restigouche, Gatineau, Kootenay, Terra Nova (conversions), St Croix, Chaudière, Columbia (standard). The last trio are similar but the four conversions all vary in silhouette. All classified as destroyer escorts (DDE) by RCN.

TYPE: FRIGATE

CLASS: 'ST LAURENT' CANADA

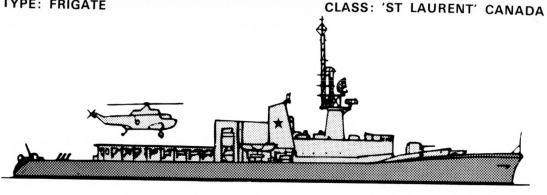

366	275	183	91	FEET
111·5	84	56	28	0 METRES

Displacement, tons: 2 260 standard, 2 800 full load
Dimensions, metres: 111·5 × 12·8 × 4 (366 × 42 × 13·2 ft)
Aircraft: 1 A/S helicopter
Guns: 2—3 in (1 twin) AA
A/S weapons: 1 mortar Mk 10 aft

Main machinery: English Electric geared turbines, 30 000 shp; 2 shafts
Speed, knots: 28·5
Complement: 250
Building dates: 1950-57

NOTES: In service in: Canada (7) St Laurent, Assiniboine, Ottawa, Saguenay, Skeena, Fraser, Margaree. *The first major warships designed in Canada. All fitted with helicopter hangars. All classified as destroyer escorts (DDH ex-DDE) in RCN.*

TYPE: FRIGATE

CLASS: 'HVIDBJØRNEN' DENMARK 141

| 238·2 | 178 | 119 | 59 | FEET |
| 72·6 | 54 | 36 | 18 | METRES | 0 |

Displacement, tons: 1 345 standard, 1 650 full load
Dimensions, metres: 72·6 × 11·6 × 4·9 (238·2 × 38 × 16 ft)
Aircraft: 1 Alouette III helicopter
Guns: 1—3 in
Main machinery: 4 GM 16-567C diesels, 6 400 bhp; 1 shaft

Speed, knots: 18
Complement: 75
Range: 6 000 at 13 knots
Building dates: 1961-63

NOTES: In service in: Denmark (4) Hvidbjørnen, Fylla, Ingolf, Vaedderen. *Designed for fishery protection and surveying duties.*

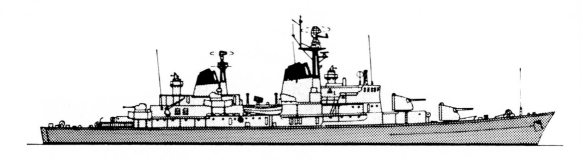

369.3	277	185	92	FEET
112.6	85	56	28	METRES 0

Displacement, tons: 2 030 standard, 2 720 full load
Dimensions, metres: 112·6 × 12 × 3·6 (369·3 × 39·5 × 11·8 ft)
Guns: 4—5 in, 4—40 mm
A/S weapons: DC
Main machinery: CODAG, 2 shafts, 2 GM 16-567 D diesels, 4 800 hp; 2 Pratt & Whitney PWA GG

4A-3 gas turbines, 44 000 hp total output
Speed, knots: 29 (18 economical)
Complement: 112
Building dates: 1964-67

NOTES: In service in: Denmark (2) Peder Skram, Herluf Trolle.

338	254	169	85	FEET
103	77	51	26	METRES 0

Displacement, tons: 1 750 standard, 1 950 full load
Dimensions, metres: 103 × 11·5 × 4·3 (338 × 37·8 × 14·1 ft)
Aircraft: 1 light helicopter can land aft
Guns: 3—3·9 in singles (*Balny* only 2), 2—30 mm
Torpedo tubes: 6—21 in ASM
A/S weapons: 1—12 in quad mortar

Main machinery: 4 SEMT-Pielstick diesels, 16 000 bhp; 2 shafts. *Balny* and *Bory* differ
Speed, knots: 25·4
Complement: 214
Range: 4 500 at 15 knots
Building dates: 1958-69

NOTES: In service in: France (9) Commandant Rivière, Amiral Charner, Balny, Commandant Bory, Commandant Bourdais, Doudart De La Grée, Enseigne De Vaisseau Henry, Protet, Victor Schoelcher. *All built by Lorient dockyard.*

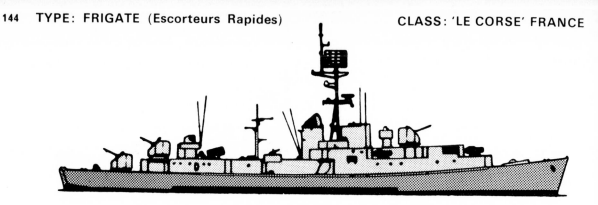

325·5	245	163	82	FEET
99·2	75	50	25	METRES 0

Displacement, tons: 1 290 standard, 1 680 full load
Dimensions, metres: 99·2 × 10·3 × 4·1 (325·5 × 33·8 × 13·5 ft)
Guns, AA: 6—57 mm (3 twin), 2—20 mm
Torpedo tubes: 12 ASM tubes (4 triple mounts forward) for homing torpedoes
A/S weapons: 2 mortars, 1 DC rack, 1 sextuple *lance roquettes*

Main machinery: Rateau A & C de B geared turbines, 20 000 shp
Speed, knots: 28·5 max, economical 14
Complement: 174
Range: 4 500 at 15 knots
Building dates: 1951-56

NOTES: *In service in:* France (4) Le Corse, Le Bordelais, Le Boulonnais, Le Brestois. *See 'Le Normand' class notes.*

325·8	245	163	82	FEET	0
99·3	75	50	25	METRES	

Displacement, tons: 1 295 standard, 1 795 full load
Dimensions, metres: 99·3 × 10·3 × 4·1 (325·8 × 33·8 × 13·5 ft)
Guns, AA: 6—57 mm in twin mountings, 2—20 mm
Torpedo tubes: 12 ASM (4 triple mountings aft)
A/S weapons: Sextuple Bofors ASM Hedgehog type or 1—12 in quad mortar; 2 DC mortars, 1 DC rack

Main machinery: Parsons or Rateau geared turbines, 20 000 shp
Speed, knots: 28
Complement: 175
Range: 4 500 at 15 knots
Building dates: 1953-60

NOTES: In service in: France (14) Le Normand, Le Lorrain, Le Picard, Le Gascon Le Champenois, Le Savoyard, Le Bourguignon, Le Breton, Le Basque, L'Agenais, Le Béarnais, L'Alsacien, Le Provencal, Le Vendéen. Similar to 'Le Corse' class (E50) except for A/S tubes aft and Hedgehog or howitzer forward.

CLASS: 'KÖLN' WEST GERMANY

360·9	269	180	90	FEET
110	82	55	27	METRES 0

Displacement, tons: 2 100 standard, 2 550 full load
Dimensions, metres: 110 × 11 × 3·4 (360·9 × 36·1
  × 11·2 ft)
Guns, AA: 2—3·9 in, 6—40 mm (2 twin, 2 single)
Torpedo tubes: 2 for ASW torpedoes
A/S weapons: 2 Bofors 4-barrelled DC mortars (rocket
  launchers)
Main machinery: Combined diesel and gas turbine

plant; 4 MAN 16-cyl diesels, total 12 000 bhp;
2 Brown-Boveri gas turbines, 26 000 bhp; total
38 000 bhp; 2 shafts
Speed, knots: 27
Complement: 210
Range: 920 at full power
Building dates: 1958-64

NOTES: In service in: West Germany (6) *Köln, Augsburg, Braunschweig, Emden, Karlsruhe, Lübeck. All built
by Stülcken of Hamburg.*

323·5	244	162	82	FEET
98·6	74	49	25	METRES 0

Displacement, tons: 2 370 standard, 2 540 full load
Dimensions, metres: 98·6 × 11·8 × 3·4 (323 5 × 38·8 × 11·2 ft)
Guns: 2—3·9 in (100 mm), 4—40 mm
Main machinery: 6 Maybach or Daimler diesels, diesel electric drive in some, 11 400 bhp; 2 shafts

Speed, knots: 21·7 max, 15 economical
Complement: 110
Range: 3 200 at 15 knots
Building dates: Completed 1961-64

NOTES: *Rated as 'tenders' but could obviously be used in lieu of frigates.* In service in: *West Germany (13)* Rhein, Donau, Elbe, Isar, Main, Mosel, Neckar, Ruhr, Saar, Werra, Weser, Lahn, Lech. *Last two slightly larger with no main armament.*

310	233	155	77	FEET
94·4	71	47	24	METRES 0

Displacement, tons: 1 110 standard, 1 290 full load
Dimensions, metres: 94·4 × 10·4 × 3·4 (310 × 34 × 11·2 ft)
Missile launchers: 1 quintuple Seakiller SS, 1 triple Seacat AA
Guns: 1—4·5 in Mk 8 or Mk 5, 2—35 mm Oerlikon

A/S weapons: 1 Limbo 3-barrelled DC mortar
Main machinery: 2 Rolls-Royce Olympus gas turbines, 2 Paxman diesels; 2 shafts, 46 000 + 3 800 shp
Complement: 125
Speed, knots: 40 designed
Building dates: 1967-72

NOTES: In service in: Iran (4) Saam, Faramarz, Rostam, Zaal. Built by Vosper Thornycroft and Vickers.

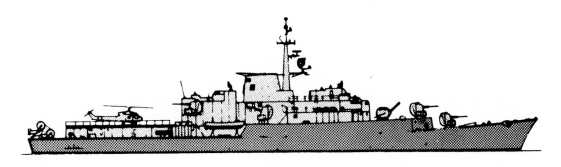

371·7	279	186	93	FEET	0
113·3	85	56	28	METRES	

Displacement, tons: 2 700 full load
Dimensions, metres: 113·3 × 13·3 × 3·9 (371·7 × 43·6 × 12·7 ft)
Aircraft: 2 A/B 204B ASW helicopters, 1 single DC mortar
Guns: 6—3 in dp single
Torpedo tubes: 6—12 in (2 triple) for A/S torpedoes
A/S weapons: 1 single DC mortar

Main machinery: 4 Tosi diesels = 16 800 hp, 2 Tosi Metrovick gas turbines = 15 000 hp; 2 shafts, 31 800 hp
Speed, knots: 22 diesel, 28 diesel and gas
Complement: 254
Range: 4 200 at 18 knots
Building dates: 1963-68

NOTES: *In service in: Italy* (2) Alpino, Carabiniere.

311·7	234	156	79	FEET
95	71	47	24	METRES 0

Displacement, tons: 1 650 full load
Dimensions, metres: 95 × 11·4 × 3·2 (311·7 × 37·4 × 10·5 ft)
Aircraft: 1 A/B-47-J3 helicopter
Guns: 2—3 in dp single
Torpedo tubes: 6—12 in (2 triple for A/S torpedoes)
A/S weapons: 1 single DC mortar

Main machinery: 4 diesels (Fiat or Tosi), 15 000 bhp; 2 shafts
Speed, knots: 26 max, 24·5 sustained
Complement: 160
Range: 4 000 at 18 knots
Building dates: 1957-62

NOTES: In service in: Italy (4) Carlo Bergamini, Carlo Margottini, Luigi Rizzo, Virginio Fasan.

338·4	254	169	85	FEET
103·1	85	57	28	METRES 0

Displacement, tons: 1 807 standard, 2 196 full load
Dimensions, metres: 103·1 × 12 × 3·8 (338·4 × 39·5 × 12·6)
Guns: 3—3 in single
Torpedo tubes: 6—12 in (2 triple) for A/S torpedoes
A/S weapons: 1 3-barrelled depth charge mortar

Main machinery: 2 double reduction geared turbines, 22 000 shp; 2 shafts
Speed, knots: 26
Complement: 255
Range: 2 500 at 20 knots
Building dates: 1952-58

NOTES: In service in: Italy (*4*) Canopo, Centauro, Cigno, Castore.

305·5	229	154	76	
93	70	47	23	FEET / METRES 0

Displacement, tons: 1 470 standard, 1 750 full load
Dimensions, metres: 93 × 10·8 × 3·5 (305·5 × 35·5 × 11·5 ft)
Guns: 2—3 in (1 twin), 2—40 mm (1 twin)
Torpedo launchers: 2 triple 12·7 in (324 mm)
A/S weapons: Octuple ASROC

Main machinery: 4 Mitsui B & W diesels, 16 000 shp; 2 shafts
Speed, knots: 25
Complement: 165
Building dates: 1968 onwards

NOTES: In service in: Japan (4) Ayase, Chikugo, Mikuma, Takashi; *5 more projected.*

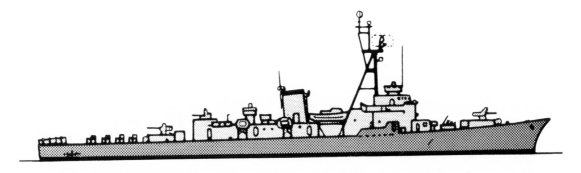

288·7   218   145   73   FEET 0
88   66   44   22   METRES

Displacement, tons: 1 070 standard, 1 300 full load
Dimensions, metres: 88 × 8·7 × 3·1 (288·7 × 28·5 × 10·2 ft)
Guns: 2—3 in dp, 2—40 mm AA
A/S weapons: 1 Hedgehog, 8 K guns; 2 DC racks
Main machinery: 12 000 hp diesels, Mitsubishi or

Mitsui B & W; 2 shafts
Speed, knots: 25
Complement: 160
Building dates: 1954-56

NOTES: In service in: Japan (2) Ikazuchi, Inazuma.

CLASS: 'VOSPER' (Mark 7) LIBYA

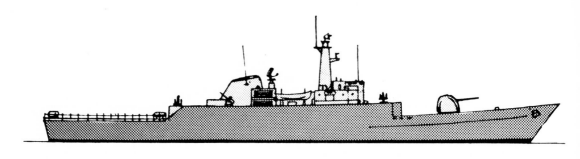

330	247	165	82	FEET
100·6	75	50	25	METRES 0

Displacement, tons: 1 325 standard, 1 625 full load
Dimensions, metres: 100·6 × 11 × 3·4 (330 × 36 × 11·2 ft)
Missile launchers: 6 Seacat (2 triple)
Guns: 1—4·5 in, 2—40 mm (twin), 2—35 mm (twin)
Main machinery: CODOG arrangement; 2 shafts; 2 Rolls-Royce gas turbines, 23 200 shp = 37·5

knots max; 2 Paxman diesels, 3 500 bhp = 17 knots
Range: 5 700 at 17 knots economical
Building dates: Scheduled to be completed in Dec 1972

NOTES: In service in: Libya (1) Dat-Assawari.

TYPE: FRIGATE

317	238	159	79	FEET	0
96·6	72	48	24	METRES	

Displacement, tons: 1 450 standard, 1 745 full load
Dimensions, metres: 96·6 × 11·2 × 5·3 (317 × 36·7 × 17·4 ft)
Missiles: Penguin to be installed in 1972
Guns: 4—3 in dp (twin mounts)
Torpedo launchers: 2

A/S weapons: Terne system
Main machinery: 1 set De Laval Ljungstrom double reduction geared turbines, 20 000 shp; 1 shaft
Speed, knots: 25
Complement: 151
Building dates: 1963-67

NOTES: In service in: Norway (5) Oslo, Bergen, Narvik, Stavanger, Trondheim.

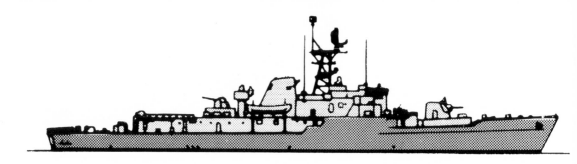

| 277·5 | 208 | 139 | 69 | FEET | 0 |
| 84·6 | 63 | 42 | 21 | METRES | |

Displacement, tons: 1 203 standard, 1 380 full load
Dimensions, metres: 84·6 × 10·3 × 3·1 (277·5 × 33·8 × 10·2 ft)
Guns: 2—3 in, 2—40 mm, AA
A/S weapons: 1 Hedgehog, 2 DC throwers, 2 DC racks
Main machinery: 2 OEW 12 cyl Pielstick diesels, 10 560 bhp

Speed, knots: 24·4
Complement: 97 plus 34 marines
Range: 5 900 at 18 knots
Building dates: Completed 1970

NOTES: In service in: Portugal (6) João Coutinho, Jacinto Candido, General Pereira D'Eca, Antonio Enes, Augusto De Castilho, Honorio Barreto. *First three built in Germany, second three in Spain, four more under construction. Officially classified as 'corvette'.*

312·5	234	156	78	FEET
95·3	72	48	24	METRES 0

Displacement, tons: 1 924 standard, 2 228 full load

Dimensions, metres: 95·3 × 12 × 5·4 (312·5 × 39·5 × 17·7 ft)

Guns, surface: 2—5 in or 6—4·7 in (3 twin) (*Gamboa*)

Guns, AA: 4—40 mm, 70 cal, or 8—37 mm (*Gamboa*); 6—20 mm

Torpedo racks: 2 side launchings for A/S

A/S weapons: 2 Hedgehogs, 8 mortars, 2 racks, or 4 DCT (*Gamboa*)

Main machinery: 2 sets Parsons geared turbines, 6 000 shp; 2 shafts

Speed, knots: 18·5

Complement: 291

Range: 4 000 at 14 knots

Building dates: 1944-51

NOTES: *In service in: Spain* (3) Legazpi, Sarmiento De Gamboa, Vicente Yañez Pinzon. Gamboa *has much heavier superstructure.*

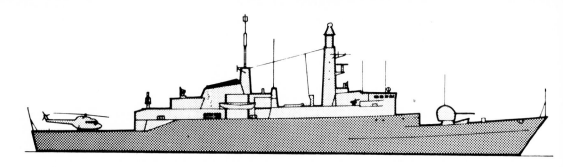

384	288	192	96	FEET
117	88	58	29	METRES 0

Displacement, tons: 2 500 full load
Dimensions, metres: 117 × 12·7 × 3·7 (384 × 41·8 × 12·3 ft)
Aircraft: 1 twin-engined Lynx A/S helicopter
Missile launchers: 1 quad Seacat
Guns: 1—4·5 in, Mk 8, 2—20 mm Oerlikon
Torpedo tubes: 6—21 inch (2 triple)
A/S weapons: Helicopter launched torpedoes

Main machinery: COGOG arrangement of 2 Rolls-Royce Olympus and 2 Tyne gas turbines, 50 000 shp; 2 shafts
Speed, knots: 30 plus
Complement: 170
Range: 4 500 at 17 knots
Building dates: 1969 onwards

NOTES: *Will be in service in: UK* (8) Amazon (*laid down Nov 1969*), Active, Ambuscade, Antelope *+4. A commercial design by Vosper Thornycroft with Yarrows.*

360	270	180	90	FEET	0
109·7	82	55	28	METRES	

Displacement, tons: 2 300 standard, 2 700 full load
Dimensions, metres: 109·7 × 12·9 × 5·3 (360 × 42·3 × 17·5 ft)
Aircraft: 1 Wasp helicopter
Missile launchers: 2 quad Seacat in *Gurkha* and *Zulu*
Guns: 2—4·5 in dp single, 2—40 mm single
A/S weapons: 1 Limbo 3-barrelled mortar

Main machinery: Combined steam and gas turbine, Metrovick steam turbine, 12 500 shp; Metrovick gas turbine, 7 500 shp; 1 shaft; total 20 000 shp
Speed, knots: 28
Complement: 253
Building dates: 1958-64

NOTES: *In service in: UK* (7) Ashanti, Eskimo, Gurkha, Mohawk, Nubian, Tartar, Zulu. Gurkha *and* Zulu *have Seacat, 2 sextuple 3-inch Mk 4 rockets and 2—20 mm.*

310	232	155	78	FEET
94·5	71	48	24	METRES 0

Displacement, tons: 1 180 standard, 1 456 full load
Dimensions, metres: 94·5 × 10·1 × 4·7 (310 × 33 × 15·5 ft)
Guns: 2—40 mm Bofors
A/S weapons: 2 Limbo 3-barrelled DC mortars
Main machinery: 1 set geared turbines, 15 000 shp; 1 shaft

Speed, knots: 27·8 max
Complement: 140
Range: 4 000 at 12 knots
Building dates: 1952-58

NOTES: In service in: UK (6) Dundas, Exmouth, Hardy, Keppel, Palliser, Russell (plus Blackwood for harbour training); India (2) Kirpan, Kuthar.

TYPE: FRIGATE

CLASS: 'LEANDER' UK
NEW ZEALAND
INDIA

372	279	186	93	FEET	0
113·4	85	56	28	METRES	

Displacement, tons: 2 450 standard, 2 860 full load
(see notes)
Dimensions, metres: 113·4 × 12·5/13·1 × 5·5 (372 ×
41/43 × 18 ft (see notes)
Aircraft: 1 Wasp helicopter armed with homing
torpedoes
Missile launchers: 1 or 2 quad Seacat or 2 sextuple
3-in Mk 4

Guns: 2—4·5 in (1 twin), 2—40 mm or 20 mm
A/S weapons: 1 Limbo 3-barrelled DC mortar
Main machinery: 2 dr geared turbines, 30 000 shp;
2 shafts
Speed, knots: 30
Complement: 263
Building dates: 1959-72

*NOTES: In service in: UK (26), New Zealand (2), India (6). See Index for names.   Last ten of UK class plus HMNZS
Canterbury have extra 65 m beam. All to be fitted with Seacat. This class is now complete, giving way to the
construction of the projected Type 22.*

CLASS: 'LEOPARD' (Type 41) UK
INDIA

339·8	248	165	83	FEET
103·6	78	52	26	METRES 0

Displacement, tons: 2 300 standard, 2 520 full load
Dimensions, metres: 103·6 × 12·2 × 4·9 (339·8 × 40 × 16 ft)
Guns: 4—4·5 in (twin), 1—40 mm
A/S weapons: 1 Squid 3-barrelled DC mortar
Main machinery: 8 ASR 1 diesels in three engine rooms, 14 400 bhp; 2 shafts, 4 engines geared to

each shaft
Speed, knots: 24
Complement: 235
Range: 7 500 at 16 knots
Building dates: 1953-59

NOTES: *Major refits for UK ships 1963-66. In service in:UK* (4) Jaguar, Leopard, Lynx, Puma; *India* (3) Beas, Betwa, Brahmaputra. *Designed for AA duties.*

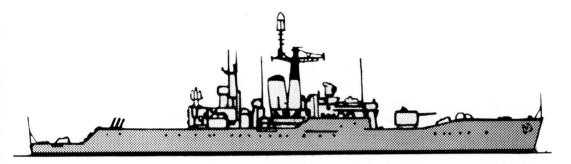

370   278   185   93   FEET
112·8   85   56   28   METRES 0

Displacement, tons: 2 380 standard, 2 800 full load
Dimensions, metres: 112·8 × 12·5 × 5·3 (370 × 41 × 17·3 ft)
Aircraft: 1 Wasp helicopter armed with homing torpedoes
Missile launchers: 1 quad Seacat, 2 sextuple 3-in Mk 4 rockets

Guns: 2—4·5 in (115 mm) (twin), 2—20 mm
A/S weapons: 1 Limbo 3-barrelled DC mortar
Main machinery: 2 double reduction geared turbines, 30 000 shp; 2 shafts
Speed, knots: 30 max
Complement: 235
Building dates: 1956-61

NOTES: In service in: UK (9) Rothesay, Berwick, Brighton, Falmouth, Londonderry, Lowestoft, Plymouth, Rhyl, Yarmouth; *with RNZN*: Otago, Taranaki.

TYPE: FRIGATE   **CLASS: 'SALISBURY' (Type 61) UK**

339·8   248   165   83   FEET   0
103·6   78   52   26   METRES

Displacement, tons: 2 170 standard, 2 408 full load
Dimensions, metres: 103·6 × 12·2 × 4·7 (339·8 × 40 × 15·5 ft)
Missile launchers: 1 quad Seacat in *Lincoln* and *Salisbury*
Guns: 2—4·5 in dp, 2—40 mm or 20 mm
A/S weapons: 1 Squid triple-barrelled DC mortar

Main machinery: 8 ASR 1 diesels in three engine rooms, 14 400 bhp; 2 shafts
Speed, knots: 24
Complement: 237
Range: 7 500 at 16 knots
Building dates: 1952-60

NOTES: In service in: UK (4) Salisbury, Llandaff, Chichester, Lincoln. *Designed for aircraft direction.*

TYPE: FRIGATE   CLASS: 'WHITBY' (Type 12) UK
INDIA

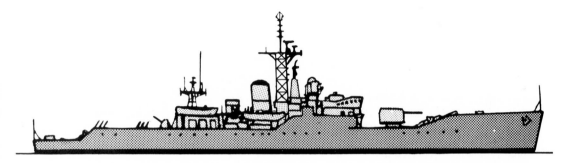

369·8	279	185	93	FEET
112·7	85	57	28	METRES	0

Displacement, tons: 2 150 standard, 2 560 full load
Dimensions, metres: 112·7 × 12·5 × 5·2 (369·8 × 41 × 17 ft)
Guns: 2—4·5 in (twin), 1 or 2—40 mm Bofors
A/S weapons: 2 Limbo 3-barrelled DC mortars

Main machinery: 2 sets dr geared turbines, 30 430 shp; 2 shafts
Speed, knots: 31
Complement: 225
Building dates: 1952-58

NOTES: In service in: UK (6) Whitby, Torquay, Tenby, Scarborough, Eastbourne, Blackpool; *India* (2) Talwar, Trishul.

TYPE: FRIGATE

**CLASS: 'BOSTWICK'
USA and others**

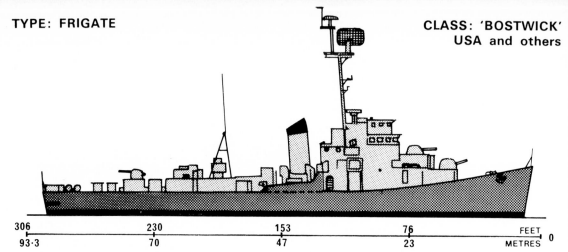

306	230	153	76	FEET
93·3	70	47	23	METRES 0

Displacement, tons: 1 240 standard, 1 900 full load
Dimensions, metres: 93·3 × 11·2 × 4·3 (306 × 37
  × 14 ft)
Guns: 3—3 in, 2—40 mm
A/S weapons: Hedgehogs, depth charges

Main machinery: Diesel electric (4 General Motors
  diesels), 6 000 shp; 2 shafts
Speed, knots: 21
Complement: 150
Building dates: Commissioned 1943-44

NOTES: In service in: USA (5), Brazil (5), France (1), Greece (4), Italy (1), Japan(2), South Korea (2), Peru (3), Philippines (1), Taiwan (4), Thailand (1), Uruguay (2). See Index for names. Classified as escort ships (DE) in USN.

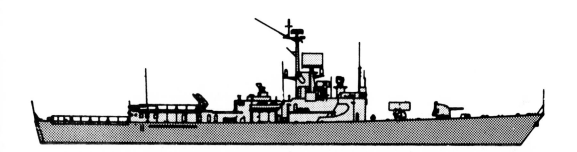

414·5		311		207		103		FEET	
126·3		95		63		31		METRES	0

Displacement, tons: 2 640 standard, 3 425 full load

Dimensions, metres: 126·3 × 13·5 × 7·3 (414·5 × 44·2 × 24 ft)

Aircraft: Facilities for small helicopter

Missiles: 1 single Tartar surface-to-air launcher ('Brooke' class)

Guns: 2—5 in dp ('Garcia' class), 1—5 in dp ('Brooke' class)

Torpedo tubes: 2 fixed (stern) (Mk 25) ('Brooke' class)

A/S weapons: 1 ASROC 8-tube launcher, 2 triple torpedo launchers (Mk 32)

Main machinery: 1 geared turbine (Westinghouse), 35 000 shp; 1 shaft

Speed, knots: 27

Complement: 241

Building dates: 1962-68

NOTES: In service in: USA (16) Brooke, Ramsey, Schofield, Talbot, Richard L Page, Julius A Furer('Brooke' class); Garcia, Bradley, Edward McDonnell, Brumby, Davidson, Voge, Sample, Koelsch, Albert David, O'Callahan ('Garcia' class). The only difference between the two classes is the Tartar system in lieu of the after 5-inch gun in the Brookes. Bronstein and McCloy are fairly similar but slightly smaller.

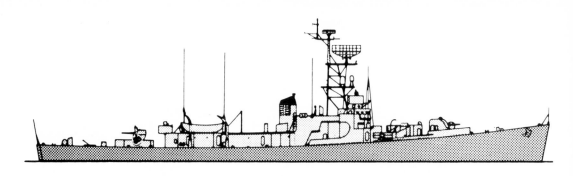

314·5	236	157	79	FEET
95·9	72	48	24	METRES 0

Displacement, tons: 1 450 standard, 1 914 full load
Dimensions, metres: 95·9 × 11·2 × 4·2 (314·5 × 36·8 × 13·6 ft)
Aircraft: Helicopter facilities in some
Guns: 4—3 in (twin) in 'Dealey' class, 2 guns in others
A/S weapons: 2 triple torpedo launchers (Mk 32)

Main machinery: 1 geared turbine (De Laval), 20 000 shp; 1 shaft
Speed, knots: 25
Complement: Approx 165
Building dates: 1952-58

NOTES: Classified as escort ships (DE) in USN. The 'Dealey' was the prototype for the first post-World War I escort ships built by the US Navy. The first two ships are known as the 'Dealey' class and the six others as the 'Courtney' class. There are five different modifications in this class. In service in: USA (8) Dealey, Hammerberg, Courtney, Lester, Evans, Bridget, Bauer, Hooper. Similar classes are 'Le Corse' and 'Le Normand' for France, 'Centauro' for Italy and 'Escobar' for Portugal built under MDAP.

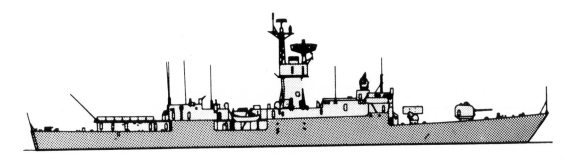

438	330	221	109	FEET
133·5	100	67	33	METRES　0

Displacement, tons: 3 011 standard, 4 100 full load
Dimensions, metres: 133·5 × 14·2 × 7·5 (438 × 46·75
　× 24·75 ft)
Aircraft: Facilities for 2 small ASW helicopters
Missiles: Space reserved for BPDMS
Guns: 1—5 in dp
A/S weapons: 1 ASROC 8-tube launcher, 4 fixed
　torpedo launchers (Mk 32)

Main machinery: 1 geared turbine (Westinghouse),
　35 000 shp; 1 shaft
Speed, knots: 27+
Complement: 220
Building dates: 1965 onwards

NOTES: In service in: USA (46). See Index for names. Classified as 'escort ships' by USN.

TYPE: FRIGATE

CLASS: 'RUDDEROW' USA
TAIWAN
SOUTH KOREA

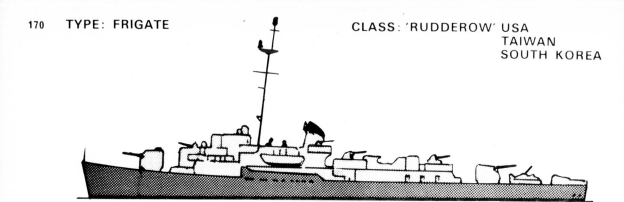

306	230	153	77	FEET
93·3	70	47	23	METRES 0

Displacement, tons: 1 450 standard, 2 230 full load
Dimensions, metres: 93·3 × 11·3 × 4·3 (306 × 37 × 14 ft)
Guns: 2—5 in dp, 4 to 8—40 mm AA
A/S weapons: Trainable Hedgehog (Mk 15) in some, DC rack

Main machinery: Turbo-electric drive (General Electric geared turbines), 12 000 shp; 2 shafts
Speed, knots: 24
Complement: 180
Building dates: Commissioned 1944

NOTES: In service in: USA (4) Hodges, Leslie L B Knox, Thomas F Nickel, Tinsman; Taiwan (1) Tai Yuan; South Korea (1) Chung Nam.

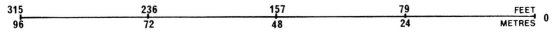

315   236   157   79   FEET   0
96   72   48   24   METRES

Displacement, tons: 1 500 standard, 1 900 full load
Dimensions, metres: 96 × 10·8 × 3·5 (315 × 35·6 × 11·5 ft)
Guns: 4—3·9 in (single), 4—37 mm
Torpedo tubes: 3—21 in (533 mm)

A/S weapons: DCTs and racks
Main machinery: Geared turbines, 30 000 shp; 2 shafts
Speed, knots: 31
Complement: 190
Building dates: 1950-52

NOTES: In service in: USSR (6)

CLASS: 'MIRKA I and II' USSR

269·9		202		135		67		FEET
82·3		61		41		20		METRES 0

Displacement, tons: 950 standard, 1 100 full load
Dimensions, metres: 82·3 × 9·1 × 3 (269·9 × 29·9 × 9·8 ft)
Guns: 4—3 in (2 twin)
Torpedo tubes: 5—16 in anti-submarine (I), 10—16 in anti-submarine (II)
A/S weapons: 4 12-barrelled rocket launchers (I), 2 16-barrelled rocket launchers (II)

Main machinery: 2 diesels, total 6 000 hp, 2 gas turbines, total 31 000 hp; 2 shafts
Speed, knots: 33
Complement: 100
Building dates: 1964 onwards

NOTES: In service in: USSR (I—21; II—4). Successors to the Petyas.

270	202	135	67	FEET
82·3	61	41	20	METRES 0

Displacement, tons: 950 standard, 1 150 full load
Dimensions, metres: 82·3 × 9·1 × 3·2 (270 × 29·9 × 10·5 ft)
Guns: 4—3 in (2 twin)
Torpedo tubes: 5—16 in A/S (I), 10—16 in A/S (II)
A/S weapons: 4 16-barrelled rocket launchers (I), 2 12-barrelled rocket launchers (II)

Main machinery: 2 diesels, total 6 000 hp; 2 gas turbines, total 30 000 hp; 2 shafts
Speed, knots: 34
Complement: 100
Building dates: 1960 onwards

NOTES: In service in: USSR (I—40 ; II—5), India (7) Kadmatt, Kamorta, Kavaratti, Katchal, Kiltan +2 recently acquired.

298·8	224	149	75	FEET
91	68	46	22	METRES 0

Displacement, tons: 1 200 standard, 1 600 full load
Dimensions, metres: 91 × 10·2 × 3·4 (298·8 × 33·7
7 × 11 ft)
Guns: 3—3·9 in (single), 4—37 mm
Torpedo tubes: 3—21 in
A/S weapons: 2 16-barrelled rocket launchers, 4 DC
  projectors

Main machinery: Geared turbines, 25 000 shp; 2 shafts
Speed, knots: 28
Complement: 150
Building dates: 1952 onwards

NOTES: In service in: USSR (48), Bulgaria (2), China (4), East Germany (2), Indonesia (7), Finland (2).

325·1	244	163	82	FEET
99·1	75	50	25	METRES 0

Displacement, tons: 1 300 standard, 1 500 full load
Dimensions, metres: 99·1 × 10·8 × 3·7 (325·1 × 35·5 × 12·2 ft)
Guns: 4—4 in (2 twin), 4—40 mm, 8—20 mm in some
A/S weapons: 2 Squids or 1 Hedgehog, 4 DCT and 2 DC racks
Torpedo tubes: 3—21 in (533 mm) (triple) in some

Main machinery: 2 sets geared turbines, 24 000 shp; 2 shafts
Speed, knots: 32 max, 28 in service
Complement: 162
Range: 3 500 at 15 knots
Building dates: 1954-57

NOTES: *In service in: Venezuela* (6) Almirante Clemente, Almirante José Garcia, Almirante Brion, General José de Austria, General José Trinidad Moran, General Juan José Flores. *All built by Ansaldo, Livorno.*

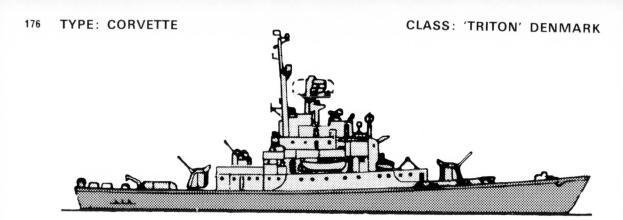

250·3	189	125	63	FEET
76·3	57	38	19	METRES 0

Displacement, tons: 760 standard, 873 full load
Dimensions, metres: 76·3 × 9·6 × 2·7 (250·3 × 31·5 × 9 ft)
Guns: 2—3 in, 1—40 mm
A/S weapons: 2 Hedgehogs, 4 DCT
Main machinery: 2 Ansaldo Fiat 409T diesels, 4 400 bhp; 2 shafts

Speed, knots: 18
Complement: 110
Range: 3 000 at 18 knots
Building dates: Launched 1954-55

NOTES: In service in: Denmark (4) Triton, Diana, Flora, Bellona.

250·3	189	125	63	FEET
76·3	57	38	19	METRES 0

Displacement, tons: 800 standard, 950 full load
Dimensions, metres: 76·3 × 9·6 × 2·8 (250·3 × 31·5 × 9·2 ft)
Guns: 2—3 in Oto Melara
Torpedo tubes: 2 triple A/S to be fitted
A/S weapons: 2 Hedgehogs Mk 2, 2 DCT, 1 DC rack

Main machinery: 2 Fiat diesels, 5 200 bhp; 2 shafts
Speed, knots: 19
Complement: 109
Range: 3 000 at 18 knots
Building dates: Commissioned 1955-56

NOTES: In service in: Italy (4) Albatros, Airone, Alcione, Aquila. *Similar to Danish 'Triton' class.*

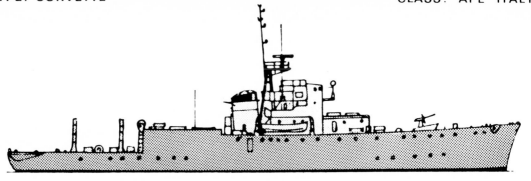

212·6	159	106	53	FEET
64·8	49	32	16	METRES 0

Displacement, tons: 670 standard, 771 full load
Dimensions, metres: 64·8 × 8·7 × 2·7 (212·6 × 28·5 × 8·9 ft)
Guns: 2 or 4—40 mm, 2—20 mm in *Bombarda*
A/S weapons: 1 Hedgehog Mk 10

Main machinery: 2 Fiat diesels, 3 500 bhp: 2 shafts
Speed, knots: 15
Complement: 100-108
Range: 2 800 at 15 knots
Building dates: Completed 1951-53

NOTES: In service in: Italy (3+1) Bombarda, Chimera, Sfinge. Ape *now used as support ship for swimmers and commandos.*

263·2	198	132	66	FEET	0
80·2	60	40	20	METRES	

Displacement, tons: 850 standard, 940 full load
Dimensions, metres: 80·2 × 10·3 × 2·7 (263·2 × 33·7
  × 9 ft)
Guns: 2—3 in single
Torpedo tubes: 2 triple for A/S torpedoes
A/S weapons: 1 single-barrelled DC mortar

Main machinery: 2 diesels, 8 400 bhp; 2 shafts
Speed, knots: 23·5 max, 21·5 sustained sea
Complement: 131
Range: 4 000 at 18 knots
Building dates: 1962-66

NOTES: *In service in: Italy (4)* Licio Visintini, Pietro De Cristofaro, Salvatore Todaro, Umberto Grosso. *Improved 'Albatros' class.*

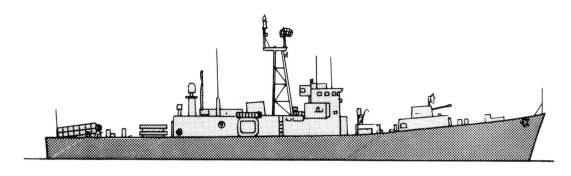

197	148	99	50	FEET 0
60	45	30	15	METRES

Displacement, tons: 420/450 standard
Dimensions, metres: 60 × 7·1 × 2·2 (197 × 23·3 × 7·5 ft)
Guns: 2—40 mm AA (twin)
A/S weapons: 1 Hedgehog, 1 DC rack, 6 homing torpedo launchers (triple)

Main machinery: 2 MAN diesels, 3 800 bhp: 2 shafts
Speed, knots: 20
Complement: 80
Building dates: 1959-66

NOTES: In service in:Japan(10) Hatsukari, Hiyodori, Kasasagi, Kumataka, Mizutori, Otori, Shiratori, Umidori, Waka-taka, Yamadori.

TYPE: CORVETTE

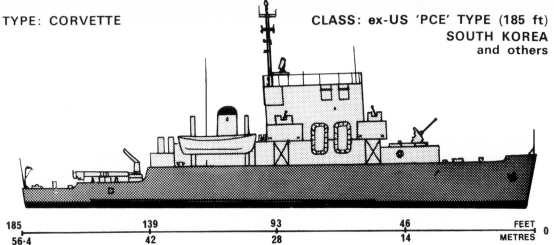

185	139	93	46	FEET
56·4	42	28	14	METRES 0

Displacement, tons: 640 standard, 903 full load
Dimensions, metres: 56·4 × 10 × 2·9 (185 × 33 × 9·5 ft)
Guns: 1—3 in 50 cal dp, 6—20 mm AA
Main machinery: GM diesels, 2 000 bhp; 2 shafts

Speed, knots: 15
Complement: 90
Building dates: 1942 onwards

NOTES: In service in: Philippines (5), South Vietnam (3), South Korea (8), Taiwan (1), Cuba (2), Ecuador (2).

TYPE: CORVETTE   **CLASS: Mk 3 VOSPER THORNYCROFT TYPE** ('Dorina')
NIGERIA

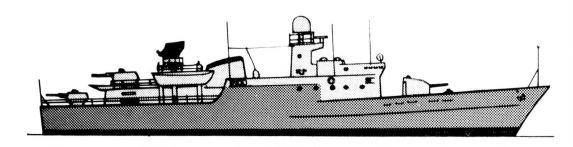

200·8	151	100	50	FEET
61·2	46	31	15	METRES 0

Displacement, tons: 500 standard, 600 full load
Dimensions, metres: 61·2 × 9·1 × 3·4 (200·8
  × 29·9 × 11·3 ft)
Guns: 2—4 in (twin), 2—40 mm Bofors (single)
Main machinery: 2 MAN diesels

Speed, knots: 26
Complement: 66
Range: 3 500 at 14 knots
Building dates: 1970 onwards

NOTES: For service in: Nigeria (2) *Dorina, Otobo.*

247·8	186	124	64	FEET
75·5	57	38	19	METRES 0

Displacement, tons: 1 031 standard, 1 135 full load
Dimensions, metres: 75·5 × 10·2 × 3 (247·8 × 33·5 × 9·8 ft)
Guns: 1—3 in, 3—40 mm
A/S weapons: 2 Hedgehogs, 8 mortars, 2 DC racks
Mines: 20 can be carried

Main machinery: Sulzer diesels, 3 200 bhp; 2 shafts
Speed, knots: 18·5 max
Complement: 113
Range: 8 000 at 10 knots
Building dates: 1950-60

NOTES: In service in: Spain (5) Atrevida, Diana, Nautilus, Princesa, Villa De Bilbao.

TYPE: CORVETTE

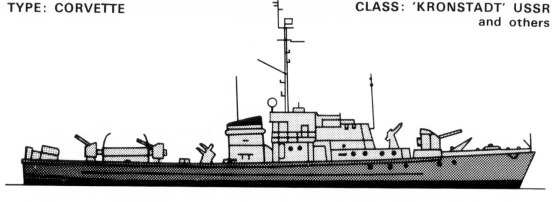

170·6	128	85	43	FEET
52	39	26	13	METRES 0

Displacement, tons: 310 standard, 380 full load
Dimensions, metres: 52 × 6·5 × 2·8 (170·6 × 21·5 × 9 ft)
Guns: 1—3·9 in, 2—37 mm, AA
A/S weapons: Depth charge projectors

Main machinery: 3 diesels, 3 300 bhp; 3 shafts
Speed, knots: 24
Complement: 65
Building dates: 1948-56

NOTES: In service in: USSR (65), Bulgaria (2), China (24), Cuba (18), Indonesia (14), Poland (8), Romania (3)

195·2	147	98	49	FEET 0
59·5	45	30	15	METRES

Displacement, tons: 550 standard, 650 full load
Dimensions, metres: 59·5 × 7·9 × 2·7 (195·2 × 26·2 × 9·2 ft)
Guns: 2—57 mm AA (1 twin mounting)
Torpedo tubes: 4—16 in anti-submarine

A/S weapons: 2 12-barrelled rocket launchers
Main machinery: 2 gas turbines, 2 diesels, 20 000 hp; 4 shafts
Speed, knots: 28
Building dates: Under construction since 1961

NOTES: In service in: USSR (75). The 750-ton 'Grisha' class with SAN-4 missiles is probably a larger development of this class.

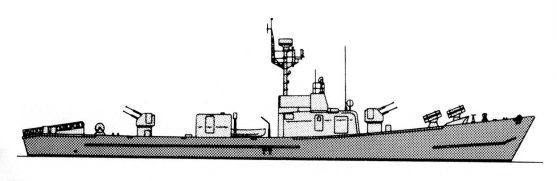

138·6	103	69	35	FEET
42	31	21	11	METRES 0

Displacement, tons: 215 light, 250 normal
Dimensions, metres: 42 × 6 × 2·9 (138·6 × 20 × 9·2 ft)
Guns: 4—25 mm AA (2 twin mountings)
A/S weapons: 4 5-barrelled ahead throwing rocket launchers

Main machinery: 3 diesels, 6 000 bhp
Speed, knots: 29
Complement: 30
Building dates: 1957 onwards

NOTES: In service in: USSR (100) (modernized version has 2—25 mm guns and 4—16 in A/S torpedo tubes); Bulgaria (6). Cuba (12). Egypt (12), East Germany (12).

TYPE: CORVETTE (FAST) CLASS: 'STENKA' USSR

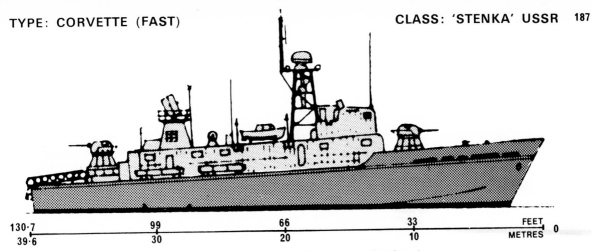

130·7	99	66	33	FEET
39·6	30	20	10	METRES 0

Displacement, tons: 170 standard, 210 full load
Dimensions, metres: 39·6 × 7·6 × 1·7 (130·7 × 25·1 × 6 ft)
Guns: 4—30 mm AA (2 twin)
Torpedo tubes: 4—16 in (406 mm) anti-submarine

A/S weapons: 2 DC racks
Main machinery: 3 diesels, 10 000 bhp
Speed, knots: 40
Complement: 25
Building dates: 1967 onwards

NOTES: In service in: USSR (30). Very difficult to classify because of their high speed.

CLASS: 'TYPE 143' WEST GERMANY

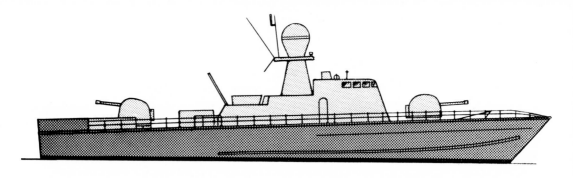

200	151	100	50	FEET
61	46	30	15	METRES 0

Displacement, tons: 360 nominal, 550 full load
Dimensions, metres: 61 × 7·5 × 2·6 (200 × 24·6 × 8·5 ft)
Guided weapons: 4 launchers for Exocet surface-to-surface missiles
Guns: 2—76 mm AA (Oto Melara)

Torpedo tubes: 2—21 in wire guided
Main machinery: 4 MTU diesels; 4 shafts
Speed, knots: 38
Complement: 40
Building dates: To be completed from 1975 onwards

NOTES: Will be in service in: West Germany (10) from 1975. Type 148 (20 craft), slightly smaller, with 4 Exocet and lattice mast in place of radome, will enter service from 1973.

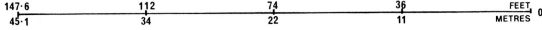

147·6	112	74	36	FEET
45·1	34	22	11	METRES 0

Displacement, tons: 220 standard, 250 full load
Dimensions, metres: 45·1 × 7 × 2·1 (147·6 × 23 × 7 ft)
Missile launchers: Up to 8 Gabriel surface-to-surface
Guns: 40 mm or 76 mm AA
Torpedo tubes: 2 side launchers for 21-in torpedoes

Main machinery: 4 Maybach diesels, 13 500 bhp; 4 shafts
Speed, knots: 40+
Complement: 35-40
Range: 2 500 at 15 knots
Building dates: 1965-70

NOTES: In service in: Israel (12). Built in France.

TYPE: MISSILE BOAT

CLASS: 'PERKASA' MALAYSIA

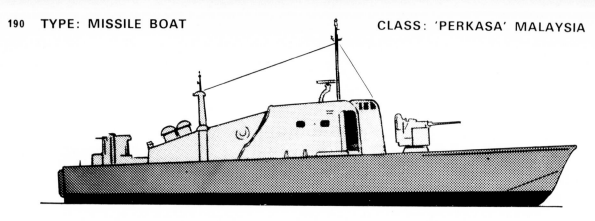

99	73	49	23	FEET
30	22	15	7	METRES 0

Displacement, tons: 95 standard, 114 full load
Dimensions, metres: 30 × 7·7 × 2·1 (99 × 25·5 × 7 ft)
Missiles: 8—SS 12(M) in 2 quad launchers
Guns: 1—40 mm, 1—20 mm, AA

Main machinery: 3 Rolls-Royce Proteus gas turbines,
 12 750 bhp; cruising diesels; 3 shafts
Speed, knots: 54
Building dates: 1964-67

NOTES: In service in: Malaysia (4) Gempita, Handalan, Pendekar, Perkasa. Built by Vosper for various roles—missile, gunboat or minelaying.

| 120 | | 90 | | 60 | | 30 | | FEET | 0 |
| 36·5 | | 27 | | 18 | | 9 | | METRES | |

Displacement, tons: 100 standard, 125 full load
Dimensions, metres: 36·5 × 6·2 × 1·5 (120 × 20·5 × 5 ft)
Missile launchers: 4 Penguin SSM
Guns: 1—40 mm
Torpedo tubes: 4—21 in

Main machinery: 2 Maybach diesels, 7 200 bhp; 2 shafts
Speed, knots: 32
Complement: 18
Building dates: Completed 1970 onwards

NOTES: In service in: Norway (6) Kjapp, Kvikk, Rapp, Rask, Snar, Snögg.

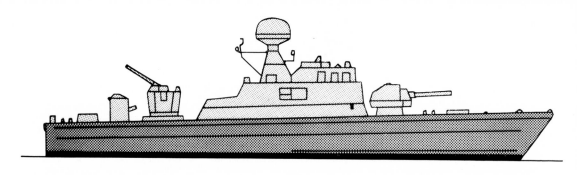

120	90	60	30	FEET
36·5	27	18	9	METRES 0

Displacement, tons: 100 standard, 125 full load
Dimensions, metres: 36·5 × 6·2 × 1·5 (120 × 20 5 × 5 ft)
Missile launchers: 6 Penguin SSM
Guns: 1—3 in, 1—40 mm

A/S weapons: DC throwers
Main machinery: 2 Maybach diesels. 7 200 bhp 2 shafts
Speed, knots: 32
Building dates: Completed 1965 onwards

NOTES: In service in: Norway (20). See Index for names.

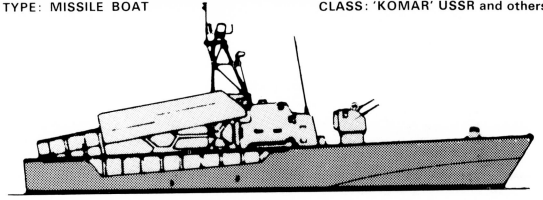

| 83·7 | | 63 | | 42 | | 20 | | FEET |
| 25·5 | | 19 | | 13 | | 6 | | METRES 0 |

Displacement, tons: 70 standard, 80 full load
Dimensions, metres: 25·5 × 6 × 1·5 (83·7 × 19·8 × 5 ft)
Missile launchers: 2 for SS-N-2A missiles

Guns: 2—25 mm AA (1 twin forward)
Main machinery: 4 diesels, 4 800 bhp; 4 shafts
Speed, knots: 40
Building dates: Since 1960-61

NOTES. In service in: USSR (25), China (3), Cuba (18), Egypt (7), Indonesia (12), Syria (8).

196·8		147		98		49		FEET
60		45		30		15		METRES 0

Displacement, tons: 800 normal
Dimensions, metres: 60 × 12 × 3 (196·8 × 39·6
   × 9·9 ft)
Missile launchers: 6 (2 triple) for SSN9 surface-to-
   surface missiles (forward) and SAN 4 launcher
Guns: 2—57 mm AA (1 twin)

A/S weapons: 1 or 2 ASW rocket launchers
Main machinery: Diesels
Speed, knots: 30
Building dates: 1969 onwards

NOTES: In service in: USSR (4). A radical change, bringing a long-range missile to sea in a fast vessel with good sea-keeping qualities and good AA defence.

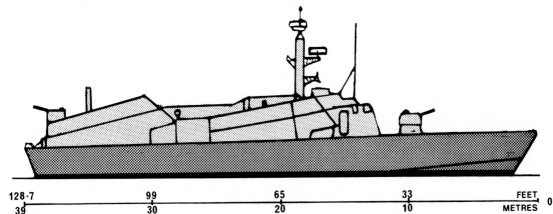

128·7	99	65	33	FEET	0
39	30	20	10	METRES	

Displacement, tons: 165 standard, 200 full load
Dimensions, metres: 39 × 7·6 × 1·8 (128·7 × 25·1 × 5·9 ft)
Missile launchers: 4 in two pairs abreast for SS-N-2A and 2B

Guns: 4—30 mm (2 twin, 1 forward, 1 aft)
Main machinery: 3 diesels, 13 000 bhp
Speed, knots: 32
Building dates: 1959 onwards

NOTES: In service in: USSR (100), China (7), Cuba (2), Egypt (12), East Germany (12), India (8), Poland (12), Romania (5).

TYPE: TORPEDO BOAT   **CLASS: 'JAGUAR' (Types 140 and 141)**
                                                                    WEST GERMANY

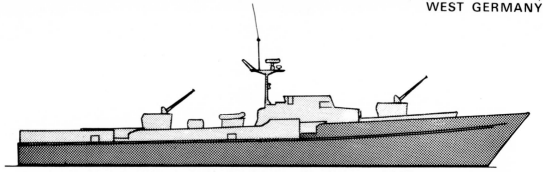

138	103	69	34	FEET
42	31	21	10	0 METRES

Displacement, tons: 160 standard, 190 full load
Dimensions, metres: 42 × 7 × 2·3 (138 × 23 × 7·5 ft)
Guns: 2—40 mm AA Bofors L 70 (single)
Torpedo tubes: 4—21 in (2 torpedo tubes can be removed for 4 mines)

Main machinery: Mercedes-Benz 20-cyl or Maybach 16-cyl diesels, 12 000 bhp; 4 shafts
Speed, knots: 42
Complement: 38
Building dates: 1958-64

NOTES: In service in: West Germany (30), 20 Type 140 with M-B diesels and 10 Type 141 with Maybach engines.

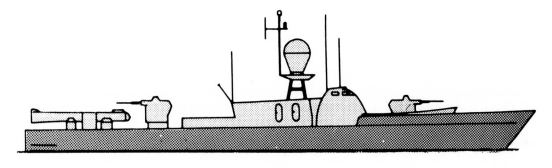

138	103	69	34	FEET	0
42	31	21	10	METRES	

Displacement, tons: 225 full load
Dimensions, metres: 42 × 7 × 2·3 (138 × 23 × 7·5 ft)
Guns: 2—40 mm AA Bofors L 70 (single)
Torpedo tubes: 2—21 in wire guided

Main machinery: 4 Mercedes-Benz 20-cyl diesels,
12 000 bhp; 4 shafts
Speed, knots: 40
Complement: 38

NOTES: *Converted from 'Jaguar' class. In service in: West Germany (10).*

CLASS: 'FALKEN' DENMARK

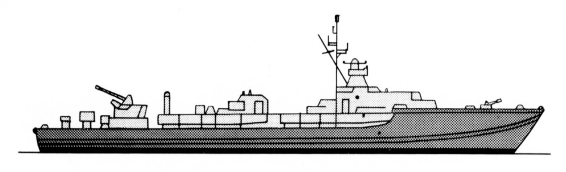

118	90	60	30	FEET 0
35·9	27	18	9	METRES

Displacement, tons: 119
Dimensions, metres: 35·9 × 5·3 × 1·8 (118 × 17·8 × 6 ft)
Guns: 1—40 mm AA, 1—20 mm AA
Torpedo tubes: 4—21 in (side)

Main machinery: 3 diesels, 9 000 bhp, 3 shafts
Speed, knots: 40
Complement: 23
Building dates: 1960-63

NOTES: In service in: Denmark (4) Falken, Glenten, Gribben, Høgen. Built in Copenhagen.

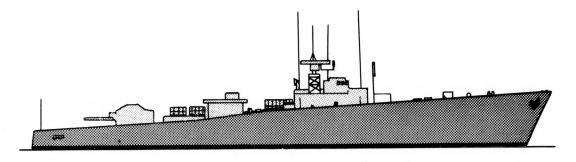

120	90	60	30	FEET
36·5	27	18	9	METRES 0

Displacement, tons: 110
Dimensions, metres: 36·5 × 5·4 × 1·8 (120 × 18 × 6 ft)
Guns: 1—40 mm, 1—20 mm, AA
Torpedo tubes: 2—21 in

Main machinery: 3 diesels, 7 500 bhp; 3 shafts
Speed, knots: 40
Complement: 22
Building dates: 1953-56

NOTES: *In service in Denmark* (6) *Flyvefisken, Hajen, Havkatten, Laxen, Makrelen, Svaerdfisken. All Danish built.*

TYPE: TORPEDO BOAT

CLASS: 'SØLØVEN' DENMARK

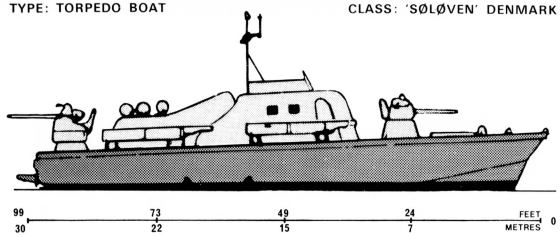

99	73	49	24	FEET
30	22	15	7	METRES 0

Displacement, tons: 95 standard, 114 full load
Dimensions, metres: 30 × 7·8 × 2·1 (99 × 25·5 × 7 ft)
Guns: 2—40 mm Bofors AA
Torpedo tubes: 4—21 in (side)
Main machinery: 3 Bristol Siddeley Proteus gas
turbines, 12 750 bhp; 3 shafts; cruising diesels
= 10 knots
Speed, knots: 54
Complement: 29
Building dates: 1962-67

NOTES: In service in: Denmark (6) Søløven, Søridderen, Søbjornen, Søhesten, Søhunden, Soulven. *First pair built by Vospers, remainder in Copenhagen.*

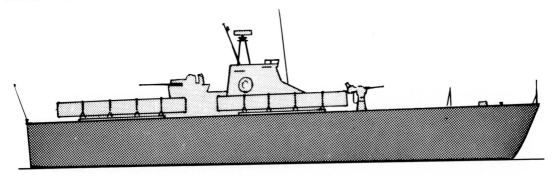

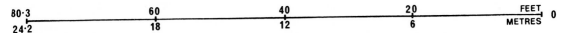

80·3   60   40   20   FEET 0
24·2   18   12   6   METRES 0

Displacement, tons: 70 standard, 82 full load
Dimensions, metres: 24·2 × 7·4 × 2·1 (80·3 × 24·5 × 6·8 ft)
Guns: 1—40 mm, 1—20 mm, AA
Torpedo tubes: 4—21 in
Main machinery: 2 Napier Deltic Turboblown diesels, 6 200 bhp; 2 shafts

Speed, knots: 45
Complement: 18
Range: 450 at 40 knots, 600 at 25 knots
Building dates: 1960-66

NOTES: In service in: Norway (20). Built in Oslo. See Index for names.

CLASS: 'SPICA' SWEDEN

143·7   108   72   36   FEET   0
43·8   33   22   11   METRES

Displacement, tons: 200 standard, 230 full load
Dimensions, metres: 43·8 × 7·1 × 1·6 (143·7× 23·3 × 5·2 ft)
Launchers: For flare rockets
Guns: 1—57 mm Bofors AA
Torpedo tubes: 6—21 in (single fixed)

Main machinery: 3 Bristol Siddeley Proteus 1 274 gas turbines, 12 750 shp; 3 shafts
Speed, knots: 40
Complement: 28
Building dates: 1965-68

NOTES: In service in: Sweden (6) Capella, Castor, Sirius, Spica, Vega, Virgo; 12 of a slightly larger successor now under construction.

TYPE: **TORPEDO BOAT**

CLASS: **'T 32' SWEDEN**

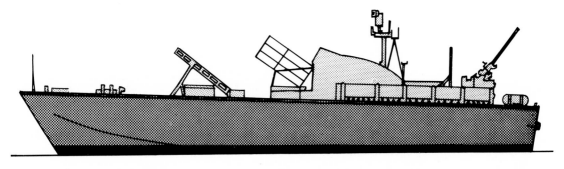

75·5	56	36	20	FEET
22·9	17	11	6	METRES 0

Displacement, tons: 40 standard
Dimensions, metres: 22·9 × 5·5 × 1·3 (75·5 × 18·4 × 4·5 ft)
Guns: 1—40 mm Bofors AA, 2 MG

Torpedo tubes: 2—21 in
Main machinery: Petrol engines
Speed, knots: 40
Building dates: 1950-53

NOTES: In service in: Sweden (10) T32-41.

TYPE: TORPEDO BOAT

CLASS: 'T 42' SWEDEN

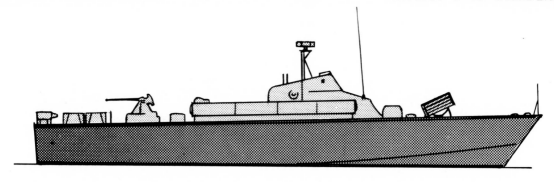

75·5		56		36		19		FEET
22·9		17		11		6		METRES 0

Displacement, tons: 40 standard
Dimensions, metres: 22·9 × 5·8 × 1·4 (75·5 × 19·4 × 4·6 ft)
Guns: 1—40 mm Bofors AA

Torpedo tubes: 2—21 in
Main machinery: Petrol engines
Speed, knots: 45
Building dates: 1955-59

NOTES: In service in: Sweden (15) T42-56.

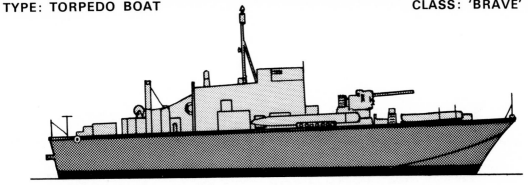

98·8	73	49	24	FEET
30	22	15	7	METRES 0

Displacement, tons: 88 standard, 114 full load
Dimensions, metres: 30 × 7·3 × 2·2 (98·8 × 24 × 7 ft)
Guns: 1 or 2—40 mm
Torpedo tubes: 2 or 4—21 in torpedoes (side launched)

Mines: Can lay mines
Main machinery: 3 Bristol Proteus gas turbines; 3 shafts
Speed, knots: 52
Complement: 20
Building dates: 1958-60

NOTES: In reserve in: UK (2) Brave Borderer, Brave Swordsman.

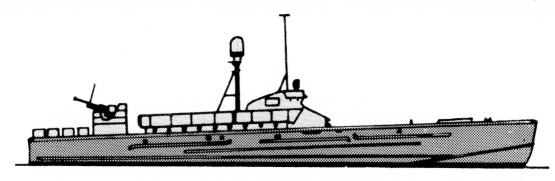

62·7	46	30	16	FEET
19	14	9	5	METRES 0

Displacement, tons: 25 normal max
Dimensions, metres: 19 × 3.5 × 1.7 (62.7 × 11.6 × 5.6 ft)
Guns: 2 MG (1 twin)

Torpedo tubes: 2—18 in
Main machinery: 2 diesels, 2 200 bhp; 2 shafts
Speed, knots: 50
Building dates: Launched 1951-58

NOTES: In service in: USSR (20), Bulgaria (8), China (70), Cuba (12), Romania (8), Syria (15).

TYPE: TORPEDO BOAT

CLASS 'P 6' 'P 8' 'P 10' USSR
CHINA and others

84·2	63	43	20	FEET	0
25·5	19	13	6	METRES	

Displacement, tons: 66 standard, 75 full load
Dimensions, metres: 25·5 × 6·1 × 1·8 (84·2 × 20 × 6 ft)
Guns: 4—25 mm AA
Torpedo tubes: 2—21 in (or mines, or DC)

Main machinery: Diesels, 4 800 bhp; 4 shafts
Speed, knots: 45
Complement: 25
Building dates: Completed 1951 onwards

NOTES: P8 and P10 (later versions of P6) have gas turbines, and different bridge and funnel. P8 boats have hydrofoils. In service in: USSR (250), China (80 P6), Cuba (12 P6), Egypt (24 P6), East Germany (18 P6), Poland (20 P6), Nigeria (3 P6). In addition Chinese 'Swatow' and 'Whampoa' classes (total 90) are P6 hulls without torpedo tubes.

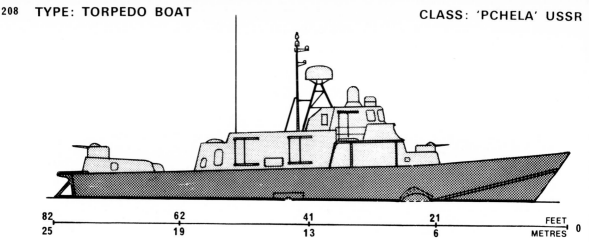

82	62	41	21	FEET
25	19	13	6	METRES 0

Displacement, tons: 70 standard, 80 full load
Dimensions, metres: 25 × 6 × ? (82 × 19·7 × ? ft)
Guns: 4 MG (2 twin)

Main machinery: Diesels, 6 000 bhp
Speed, knots: 50
Building dates: Since 1964-65
Special features: Also carry depth charges.

NOTES: In service in: USSR (25). Main class of Soviet hydrofoils.

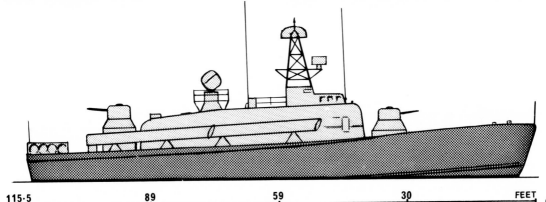

115·5	89	59	30	FEET	0
35	27	18	9	METRES	

Displacement, tons: 150 standard, 160 full load
Dimensions, metres: 35 × 7 × 1·5 (115·5 × 23·1 × 5 ft)
Guns: 4—30 mm AA (2 twin)
Torpedo tubes: 4—21 in (single)

A/S weapons: 12 DC
Main machinery: Diesels, 13 000 bhp; 3 shafts
Speed, knots: 38
Complement: 16
Building dates: 1962 onwards

NOTES: In service in: USSR (30), Egypt (6), East Germany (15).

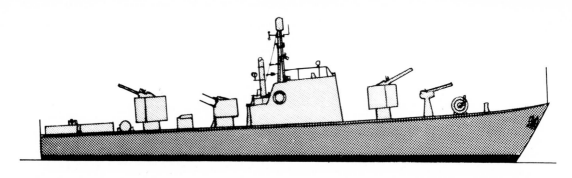

128·6	96	64	32	FEET	0
39·2	30	20	10	METRES	

Displacement, tons: 120 full load
Dimensions, metres: 39·2 × 5·4 × 1·8 (128·6 × 18 × 5·5 ft)
Missiles: 4 of Pakistan's to receive missiles
Guns: 4—37 mm (I), 4—37 mm, 4—25 mm (II)
Torpedo tubes: 2 in earlier Shanghai II

Main machinery: 4 diesels, 4 800 bhp (I), 5 000 bhp (II)
Speed, knots: 28 (I), 30 (II)
Complement: 21-25
Range: 800 at 17 knots
Building dates: 1959, continuing

NOTES: In service in: China (225), Tanzania (6), Ceylon (2 with 4 to come); planned for Pakistan (6+).

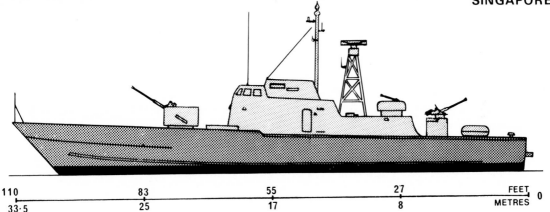

110	83	55	27	FEET	0
33·5	25	17	8	METRES	

Displacement, tons: 100 standard
Dimensions, metres: 33·5 × 6·4 × 1·9 (110 × 21 × 6·5 ft)
Guns: 1—40 mm AA (forward), 1—20 mm AA (aft)
Main machinery: 2 Maybach diesels, 2 × 3 500 bhp

Speed, knots: 32 max
Complement: 19-22
Range: Over 1 000 at 15 knots
Building dates: 1968 onwards

NOTES: In service in: Singapore (3) Independence, Freedom, Justice.

TYPE: PATROL CRAFT

**CLASS: VOSPER THORNYCROFT Type B
('Sovereignty')
SINGAPORE**

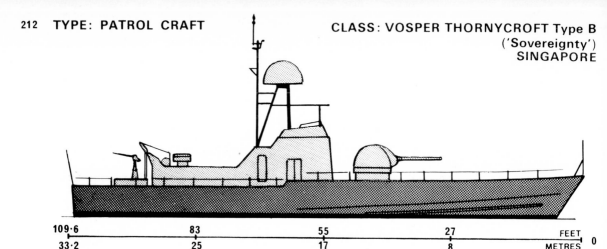

109·6	83	55	27	FEET
33·2	25	17	8	METRES 0

Displacement, tons: 100 standard, 130 full load
Dimensions, metres: 33·2 × 6·4 × 1·7 (109·6 × 21 × 5·6 ft)
Guns: 1—76 mm Bofors, 1—20 mm Oerlikon
Main machinery: 2 Maybach MD 872 diesels, 2 × 3 600 bhp

Speed, knots: 32 max
Complement: 19
Range: Over 1 000 at 15 knots
Building dates: Completed 1971 onwards

NOTES: In service in: Singapore (3) Sovereignty, Daring, Dauntless.

TYPE: PATROL CRAFT

173	129	86	43	FEET
53	39	26	13	METRES 0

Displacement, tons: 280 standard, 450 full load
Dimensions, metres: 53 × 7 × 3·2 (173 × 23 ×10·5 ft)
Guns: 1—3 in dp, 1—40 mm, 4—20 mm AA
A/S weapons: 2 DC, 2 RL

Main machinery: Diesel, 2 800 bhp; 2 shafts
Speed, knots: 19
Complement: 51
Building dates: 1944 onwards

NOTES: In service in: Cambodia (2), Indonesia (4), South Korea (3), Philippines (4), Venezuela (10), South Vietnam (1).

TYPE: PATROL CRAFT (PG)

**CLASS: 'ASHEVILLE' USA
SOUTH KOREA**

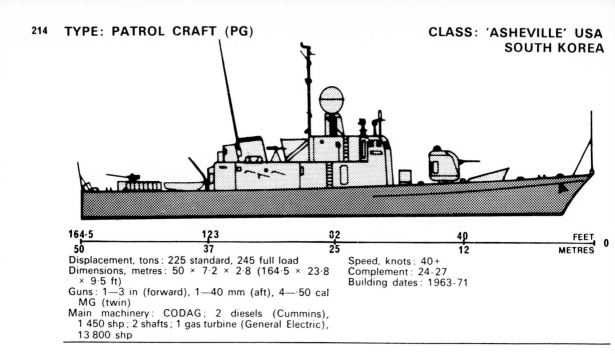

164·5	123	82	40	FEET
50	37	25	12	0 METRES

Displacement, tons: 225 standard, 245 full load
Dimensions, metres: 50 × 7·2 × 2·8 (164·5 × 23·8
  × 9·5 ft)
Guns: 1—3 in (forward), 1—40 mm (aft), 4—·50 cal
  MG (twin)
Main machinery: CODAG; 2 diesels (Cummins),
  1 450 shp; 2 shafts; 1 gas turbine (General Electric),
  13 800 shp

Speed, knots: 40+
Complement: 24-27
Building dates: 1963-71

NOTES: *In service in: USA (16)* South Korea Paek Ku. *Two craft now fitted with Standard surface-to-surface missiles.*

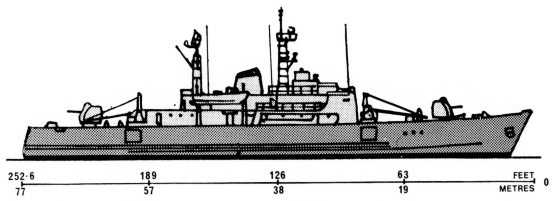

252·6   189   126   63   FEET
77   57   38   19   METRES   0

Displacement, tons: 1 900 full load
Dimensions, metres: 77 × 12·5 × 3 (252·6 × 41 × 10 ft)
Guns: 4—3 in (2 twin mountings)
Mines: 400
Main machinery: 2 GM-567D3 diesels, 4 800 shp;
   2 shafts

Speed, knots: 17
Complement: 120
Building dates: 1962-64

NOTES: In service in: Denmark (4) Falster, Fyen, Moen, Sjaelland.

CLASS: 'SOOYA' JAPAN

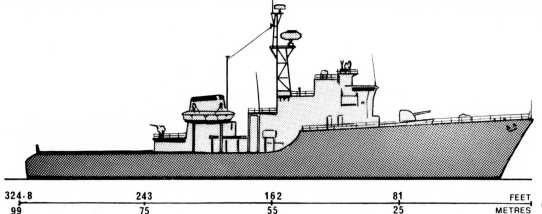

324·8	243	162	81	FEET
99	75	55	25	METRES 0

Displacement, tons: 2 150 standard
Dimensions, metres: 99 × 15 × 4·2 (324·8 × 49·2
    × 13·8 ft)
Guns: 2—3 in (1 twin), 2—20 mm
Torpedo tubes: 6 anti-submarine type (2 triple)

Mines: Could carry 200
Main machinery: 4 diesels, 6 400 bhp, 2 screws
Speed, knots: 18
Complement: 185
Building dates: Still building

NOTES: Will be in service in: Japan (1) Sooya.

TYPE: FLEET MINESWEEPER

CLASS: 'HABICHT II' 217
EAST GERMANY

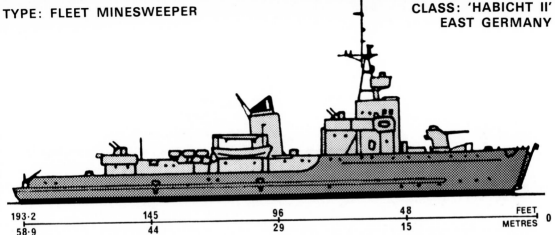

193·2	145	96	48	FEET
58·9	44	29	15	METRES 0

Displacement, tons: 550 standard
Dimensions, metres: 58·9 × 8·1 × 3·7 (193·2
× 26·5 × 11·8 ft)
Guns: 1—3·4 in, 8—25 mm AA paired vertically
A/S weapons: 4 DCT

Main machinery: 2 diesels, 2 800 bhp; 2 shafts
Speed, knots: 17
Complement: 80
Building dates: Completed 1955-56

NOTES: In service in: East Germany (2). 'Habicht II' is similar to 'Habicht I' but lengthened by 6 metres.

TYPE: FLEET MINESWEEPER

229·7	172	115	57	FEET
70	52	35	17	METRES 0

Displacement, tons: 650 standard
Dimensions, metres: 70 × 8·1 × 3·7 (229·7 × 26·5 × 12·2 ft)
Guns: 1—3·4 in, 10—25 mm AA paired vertically
A/S weapons: 4 DCT

Main machinery: Diesels, 3 400 bhp; 2 shafts
Speed, knots: 18
Complement: 90
Building dates: 1956-58

NOTES: In service in: East Germany (10).   See Index for names.

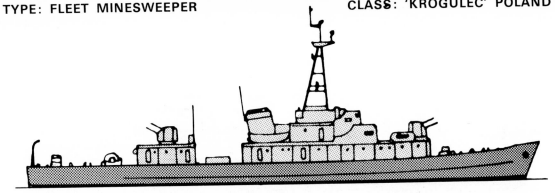

190·3	142	95	47	FEET
58	43	29	14	METRES 0

Displacement, tons: 500
Dimensions, metres: 58 × 7·5 × 2·5 (190·3 × 24·6 × 8·2 ft)
Guns: 6—25 mm AA

Main machinery: Diesels
Speed, knots: 16
Building dates: 1963 onwards

NOTES: In service in: Poland (12).   See Index for names.

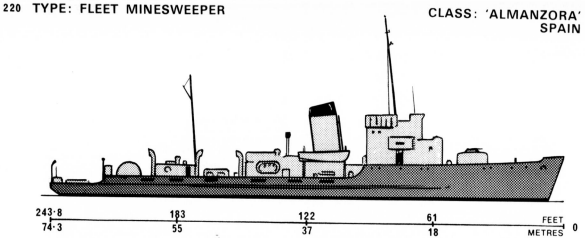

243·8		183		122		61		FEET	0
74·3		55		37		18		METRES	

Displacement, tons: 671 standard, 770 full load
Dimensions, metres: 74·3 × 10·2 × 3·7 (243·8 × 33·5 × 12·3 ft)
Guns: 2—20 mm AA
Main machinery: Triple expansion and exhaust turbines, 2 400 hp; 2 shafts

Speed, knots: 13
Complement: 79
Range: 1 000 at 6 knots
Building dates: Completed 1954, modernized 1961

NOTES: In service in: Spain (7). See Index for names.

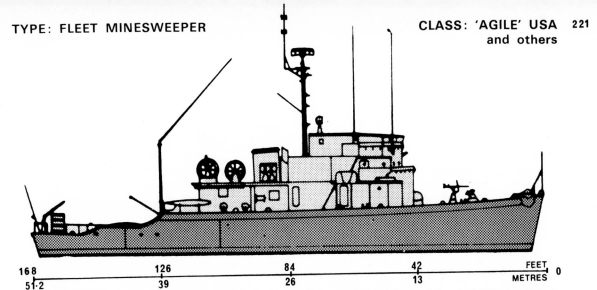

16 8		126		84		42		FEET	0
51·2		39		26		13		METRES	

Displacement, tons: 665 light, 750 full load
Dimensions, metres: 51·2 × 10·9 × 4·1 (168 × 36 × 13·6 ft)
Guns: 1—40 mm AA, 2—·50 cal MG in some, 2—20 mm in some

Main machinery: 4 Packard diesels, 2 280 bhp; 2 shafts
Speed, knots: 15·5
Complement: 72-76
Building dates: 1952-58

NOTES: In service in: USA (48), Belgium (7 'Acme' class), France (14 'Berneval' class), Italy (4), Netherlands (6, classified as support ships), Portugal (4 'Acme' class), Spain (4), Uruguay (1). See Index for names. All three classes generally similar.

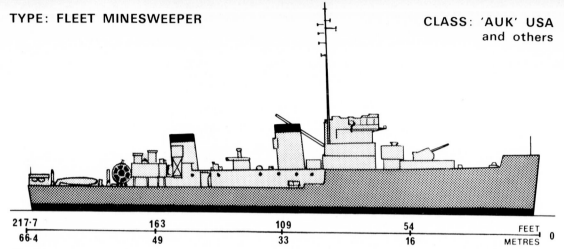

217·7	163	109	54	FEET
66·4	49	33	16	METRES

Displacement, tons: 890 standard, 1 250 full load
Dimensions, metres: 66·4 × 9·8 × 3·3 (217·7 × 32·1 × 10·8 ft)
Guns: 1—3 in dp; 2—40 mm AA (single) or 4—40 mm AA (twin)

Main machinery: Diesel electric, 3 250 bhp; 2 shafts
Speed, knots: 18
Complement: 105-117
Building dates: Completed 1942-45

NOTES: In service in: USA (25), Norway (4) (converted to minelayers), Peru (2), Korea (3), Taiwan (3), Philippines (2), Uruguay (1).

TYPE: FLEET MINESWEEPER CLASS: T 43 223

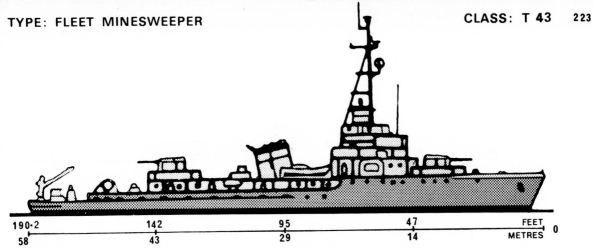

| 190·2 | 142 | 95 | 47 | FEET |
| 58 | 43 | 29 | 14 | METRES 0 |

Displacement, tons: 500 standard, 610 full load
Dimensions, metres: 58 × 8·6 × 2·1 (190·2 × 28·2 × 6·9 ft)
Guns: 4—37 mm AA (2 twin), 4—25 mm

Main machinery: 2 diesels, 2 000 bhp; 2 shafts
Speed, knots: 17
Building dates: 1948-57
Complement: 40

NOTES: In service in: USSR (120), Albania (2), Bulgaria (2), China (20), Egypt (6), Indonesia (6), Poland (12), Syria (2).

TYPE: FLEET MINESWEEPER   **CLASS: 'T 58' USSR**
INDIA

229·9	172	115	57	FEET
70·1	52	35	17	METRES 0

Displacement, tons: 790 standard, 900 full load
Dimensions, metres: 70·1 × 9·2 × 2·4 (229·9 × 29·5 × 7·9 ft)
Guns: 4—57 mm AA (2 twin)

Main machinery: 2 diesels, 4 000 bhp; 2 shafts
Speed, knots: 18
Building dates: 1957-64

NOTES: In service in: USSR (20), India (1) Nistar.

TYPE: FLEET MINESWEEPER

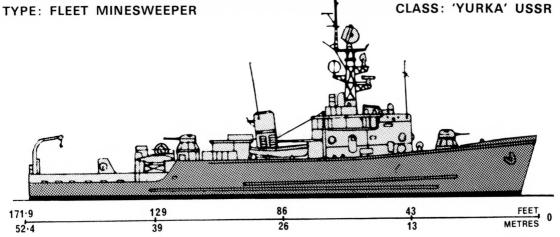

171·9		129		86		43		FEET	0
52·4		39		26		13		METRES	

Displacement, tons: 500 standard, 550 full load
Dimensions, metres: 52·4 × 9·4 × 2·7 (171·9 × 31 × 8·9 ft)
Guns: 4—30 mm AA (2 twin)

Main machinery: 2 diesels, 4 000 bhp (possibly gas turbines in lieu)
Speed, knots: 18
Building dates: 1963 onwards

NOTES: In service in: USSR (45).

TYPE: MINEHUNTER   **CLASS: 'CIRCE' FRANCE**

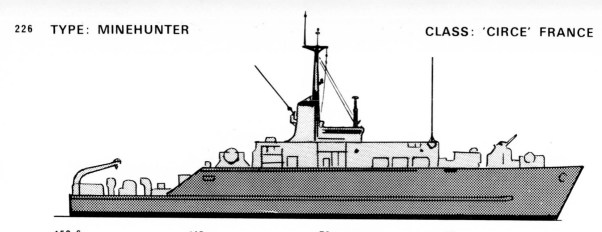

152·6	115	76	39	FEET
46·4	35	23	12	METRES 0

Displacement, tons: 460 standard, 510 full load
Dimensions, metres: 46·4 × 8·8 × 2·4 (152·6 × 29·2 × 8 ft)
Guns: 1—20 mm
Main machinery: Diesels, 1 800 bhp; single axial screw; twin active rudders

Speed, knots: 15
Complement: 50
Range: 3 000 at 12 knots
Building dates: 1968 onwards

NOTES: *In service in: France* (5) Calliope, Ceres, Circe, Clio, Cybele.

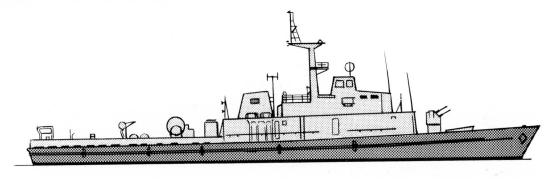

| 154·2 | | 118 | | 77 | | 39 | | FEET | 0 |
| 46·9 | | 36 | | 24 | | 12 | | METRES | |

Displacement, tons: 245 standard, 280 full load
Dimensions, metres: 46·9 × 7 × 2 (154·2 × 23 × 6·6 ft)
Guns: 2—25 mm or 2—30 mm

Main machinery: Diesels, 4 000 bhp; 2 shafts
Speed, knots: 24
Building dates: Completed 1970 onwards

NOTES: In service in: East Germany (25).   See Index for names.

TYPE: COASTAL MINESWEEPER   **CLASS: 'LINDAU' WEST GERMANY**

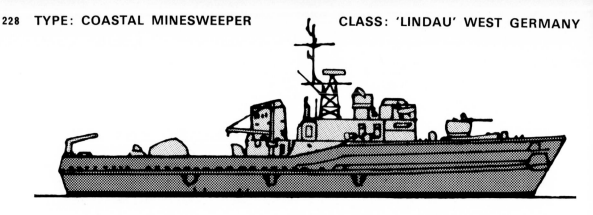

142·1	107	71	36	
43·3	33	22	11	FEET 0
				METRES

Displacement, tons: 370 standard, 425 full load
Dimensions, metres: 43·3 × 8·3 × 2·6 (142·1 × 27·2 × 8·5 ft)
Guns: 1—40 mm AA

Main machinery: Maybach diesels, 4 000 bhp; 2 shafts
Speed, knots: 17
Complement: 46
Building dates: Completed 1957-64

NOTES: In service in: West Germany (18).   See Index for names.

TYPE: **COASTAL MINESWEEPER**   CLASS: **'SCHÜTZE' WEST GERMANY**
BRAZIL

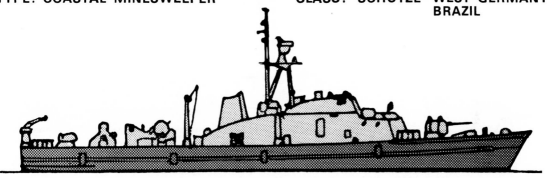

154·9		119		79		39		FEET	
47·2		36		24		12		METRES	0

Displacement, tons: 230 standard, 280 full load
Dimensions, metres: 47·2 × 7·2 × 2·1 (154·9 × 23·6 × 6·9 ft)
Guns: 1 or 2—40 mm AA

Main machinery: Maybach diesels, 4 500 bhp; 2 shafts
Speed, knots: 24
Complement: 39
Building dates: Completed 1959-64

NOTES: In service in: West Germany (28), Brazil (4).   See Index for names.

TYPE: COASTAL MINESWEEPER **CLASS: 'KASADA' JAPAN**

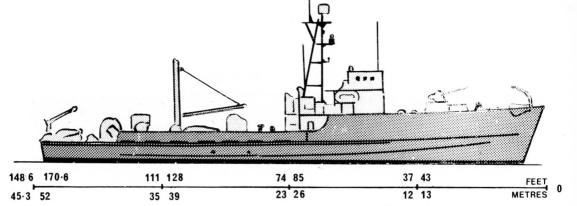

148·6 170·6   111 128   74 85   37 43   FEET
                                                                               0
45·3   52   35   39   23 26   12 13   METRES

Displacement, tons: 340/380 standard
Dimensions, metres: 45·3/52 × 8·6/9·1 × 2·3 (148·6/
  170·6 × 27·6/30 × 7·5 ft)
Guns: 1—20 mm AA

Main machinery: 2 diesels, 1 200/1 440 bhp; 2 shafts
Speed, knots: 14
Building dates: 1958-70

NOTES: In service in: Japan(34). Later ships of this class are slightly larger than the earlier ones. See Index for names.

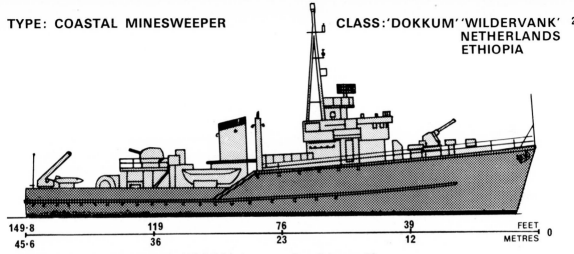

149·8		119		76		39		FEET	
45·6		36		23		12		METRES	0

Displacement, tons: 373 standard, 417 full load
Dimensions, metres: 45·6 × 8·5 × 2 (149·8 × 28 × 6·5 ft)
Guns: 2—40 mm
Main machinery: 2 diesels, Fyenoord MAN or Werk-spoor, 2 500 bhp

Speed, knots: 16
Complement: 38
Building dates: Completed 1955-56

NOTES: In service in: Netherlands (26), Ethiopia (1). See Index for names.

CLASS: 'TON' UK and others

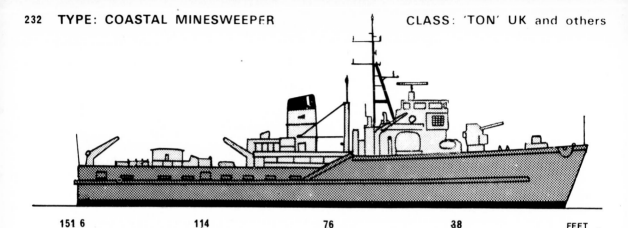

151 6	114	76	38	FEET
46·2	36	23	12	METRES 0

Displacement, tons: 360 standard, 425 full load
Dimensions, metres: 46·2 × 8·8 × 2·5 (151·6 × 28·8 × 8·2 ft)
Guns: 1—40 mm AA, 2—20 mm AA (minehunters 2—40 mm)
Main machinery: 2 diesels (Mirrlees or Deltic), 2 500 bhp; 2 shafts

Speed, knots: 15
Complement: 27 (36 in minehunters)
Range: 2 300 at 13 knots
Building dates: 1953-60

NOTES: In service in: UK (37 incl. 14 minehunters), Argentina (6), Australia (6), Ghana (1), India (4), Ireland (3), Malaysia (6), South Africa (10). Five of this class now serve in RN as coastal patrol vessels in addition to the above CMS. French 'Sirius' class and Portuguese 'San Roque' class generally similar. All names in Index.

TYPE: COASTAL MINESWEEPER **CLASS: 'WILTON' UK** 233

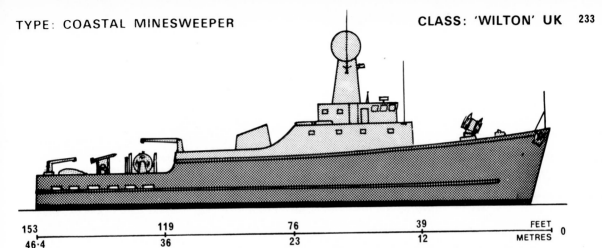

153	119	76	39	FEET
46·4	36	23	12	METRES 0

Displacement, tons: 500 standard
Dimensions, metres: 46·4 × 8·6 × 2·6 (153 × 28·8
  × 8·5 ft)
Guns: 1—40 mm

Main machinery: 2 Deltic diesels; 2 shafts
Speed, knots: 16
Complement: 37
Building dates: 1971-72

NOTES: Included as the first GRP (Glass Reinforced Plastic) warship built in the world.

TYPE: COASTAL MINESWEEPER

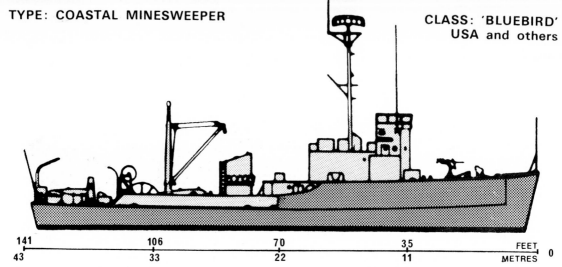

141	106	70	35	FEET
43	33	22	11	0 METRES

Displacement, tons: 320 light, 370 full load
Dimensions, metres: 43 × 8·5 × 2·5 (144 × 27·9 × 7·5 ft)
Guns: 2—20 mm AA (twin)
Main machinery: 2 GM diesels, 880 bhp; or Packard

engines, 1 200 bhp; 2 shafts
Speed, knots: 12 or 12·5
Complement: 39
Building dates: Completed 1953-56

NOTES: In service in: USA (13), Belgium (9), Denmark (8), France (27), Greece (10), Indonesia (6), Iran (4), Netherlands (14), Norway (10), Pakistan (8), Italy (18), Portugal (8), Taiwan (14), Korea (6), Philippines (2), Spain (12), Thailand (4), Turkey (12), Vietnam (2), Japan (4). See Index for names.

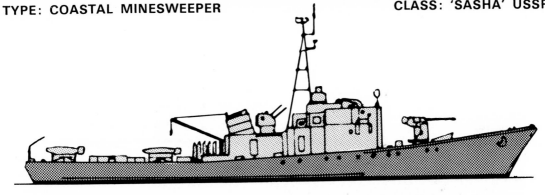

150·9	112	7·6	36	FEET 0
45·9	34	23	11	METRES

Displacement, tons: 245 standard, 280 full load
Dimensions, metres: 45·9 × 6·2 × 2 (150·9 × 20·5 × 6·6 ft)
Guns: 1—57 mm dp, 4—25 mm AA (2 twin)

Main machinery: 2 diesels, 2 200 bhp
Speed, knots: 18
Complement: 25

NOTES: In service in: USSR (35).

TYPE: COASTAL MINESWEEPER   **CLASS: 'VANYA' USSR**

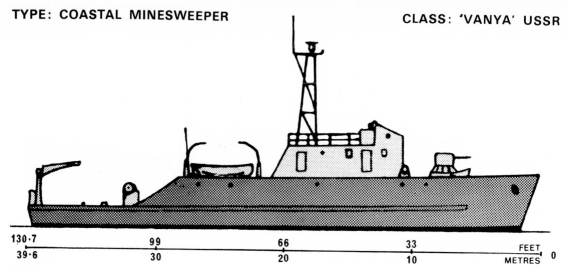

130·7	99	66	33	FEET
39·6	30	20	10	METRES 0

Displacement, tons: 250 standard, 275 full load
Dimensions, metres: 39·6 × 7·3 × 2·1 (130·7 × 24 × 6·9 ft)
Guns: 2—30 mm AA (1 twin)

Main machinery: 2 diesels, 2 200 bhp
Speed, knots: 18
Complement: 30
Building dates: 1961 onwards

NOTES: In service in: USSR (50).

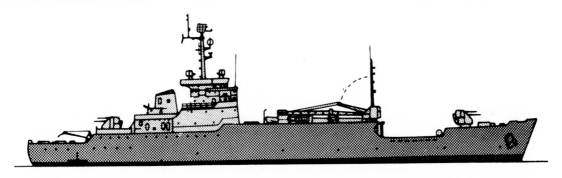

370	277	185	92	FEET
112·8	84	56	28	METRES 0

Displacement, tons: 5 000 standard, 7 000 full load
Dimensions, metres: 112·8 × 14·4 × 5·8 (370 × 47·2 × 19 ft)
Guns: 8—57 mm (2 quad, 1 on the forecastle, 1 on the break of the quarter deck)

Main machinery: Diesels, 5 000 shp; 2 shafts
Speed; knots: 15

NOTES: In service in: USSR (5). Capable of missile servicing and supply.

TYPE: SUBMARINE SUPPORT SHIP

**CLASS: 'UGRA' USSR
INDIA**

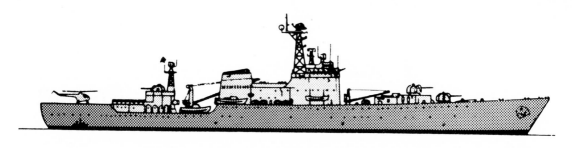

463·8	348	232	116	FEET
141·4	106	71	35	METRES 0

Displacement, tons: 6 750 standard, 9 500 full load
Dimensions, metres: 141·4 × 17·6 × 6·5 (463·8 × 57·6 × 21·3 ft)
Aircraft: Provision for helicopter
Guns: 8—2·3 in (57 mm) dp, 4 twin mounts, 2 forward, 2 aft

Main machinery: Diesels, 2 × 7 000 bhp: 2 shafts
Speed, knots: 17
Building dates: 1961-68

NOTES: In service in: USSR (5), India (1) Amba.

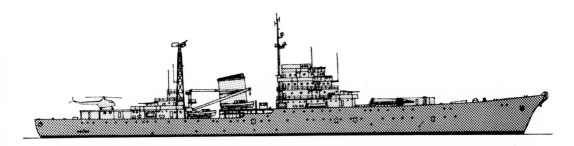

| 458·9 | 343 | 229 | 114 | FEET | 0 |
| 139·9 | 105 | 70 | 35 | METRES | |

Displacement, tons: 6 700 standard, 9 000 full load
Dimensions, metres: 139·9 × 17·6 × 6·8 (458·9 × 57·7 × 22·3 ft)
Aircraft: Provision for helicopter in two ships
Guns: 4—3·9 in (100 mm), 8—57 mm (twins)

Main machinery: 4 or 6 diesels, 14 000 bhp
Speed, knots: 21
Complement: 300
Building dates: 1957-62

NOTES: In service in: USSR (6), Indonesia (1) Ratulangi.

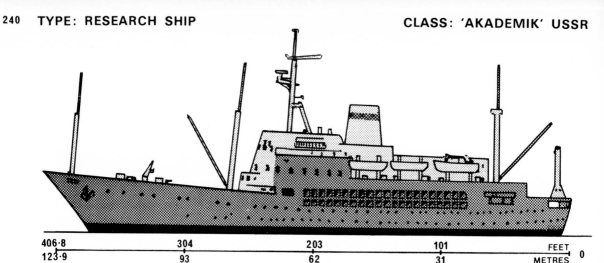

406·8	304	203	101	FEET
123·9	93	62	31	METRES 0

Displacement, tons: 6 681 full load
Dimensions, metres: 123·9 × 17 × 4·5 (406·8 × 56 × 15 ft)
Main machinery: 2 Halberstadt 6-cyl diesels, 8 000 bhp; 2 shafts

Speed, knots: 18-20
Building dates: Completed 1968

NOTES: In service in: USSR (8). Larger but still typical units of the very large Soviet oceanographic and hydrographic fleet, now numbering between 80 and 90.

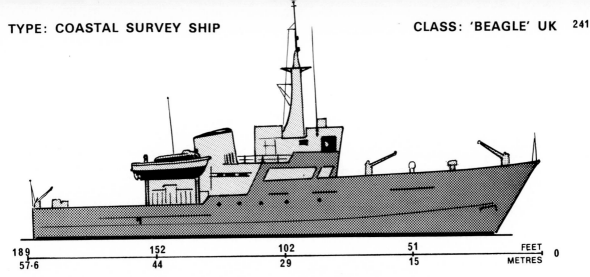

189	152	102	51	FEET	0
57·6	44	29	15	METRES	

Displacement, tons: 800 standard, 1 088 full load
Dimensions, metres: 57·6 × 11·4 × 3·6 (189 × 37·5 × 12 ft)
Main machinery: 4 Lister Blackstone diesels; 2 shafts

Speed, knots: 15
Complement: 38
Range: 4 000 at 12 knots
Building dates: 1966-68

NOTES: *In service in: UK* (4) Beagle, Bulldog, Fawn, Fox. *Specially designed for coastal survey work to replace the converted CMS class.*

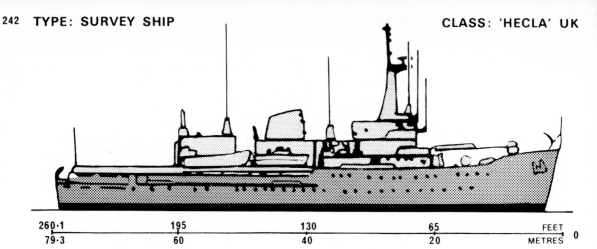

260·1	195	130	65	FEET
79·3	60	40	20	METRES 0

Displacement, tons: 1 915 light, 2 733 full load
Dimensions, metres: 79·3 × 15 × 4·7 (260·1 × 49·1 × 15·6 ft)
Aircraft: 1 Wasp helicopter
Main machinery: 3 Paxman Ventura diesels, 3 840 bhp 1 electric motor, diesel electric, 1 screw

Speed, knots: 14·5
Complement: 118
Range: 12 000 at 11 knots
Building dates: 1964–66 and 1972

NOTES: In service in: UK (3+1) Hecla, Hecate, Hydra. *First commercially designed survey ships for the RN. Dual oceanographic/hydrographic role and a great advance over the old converted warships. One modified 'Hecla'* (Herald) *under construction (1972).*

TYPE: SPACE EVENT SHIP

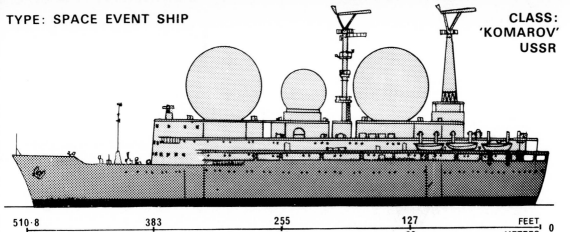

510·8	383	255	127	FEET 0
155·6	117	78	39	METRES

Displacement, tons: 17 500 full load
Dimensions, metres: 155·6 × 22·9 × 8·9 (510·8 × 75·5 × 29 ft)
Measurement, tons: 8 000 approx

Main machinery: Diesels, 24 000 bhp; 2 shafts
Speed, knots: 22
Building dates: Completed 1968

NOTES: In service in: USSR (2). Included to show the strange silhouette of this pair of unmistakable ships.

TYPE:
RESEARCH
SHIP

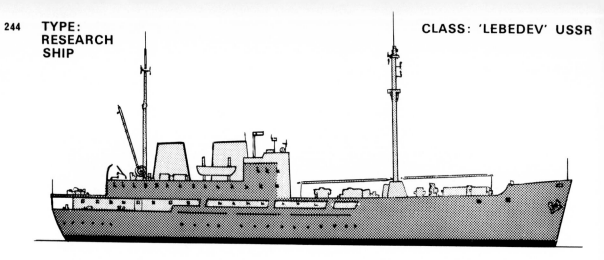

Measurement, tons: 1 180 net, 3 561 gross
Main machinery: Diesels
Building date: 1954

*NOTES: Carry comprehensive equipment and accommodation for oceanographic, acoustic and hydrological research.
In service in: USSR (2) Petr Lebedev, Sergei Vavilov, both well-known Atlantic visitors.*

246·1   185   123   62   FEET
75   57   38   19   METRES 0

Displacement, tons : 1 240 standard, 1 800 full load
Dimensions, metres : 75 × 9·9 × 4 (246·1 × 33 × 13 ft)
Main machinery : Diesels
Speed, knots : 16
Building dates : 1967 onwards

NOTES: In service in: USSR (8). One of the standard classes of survey ship in the Soviet fleet.

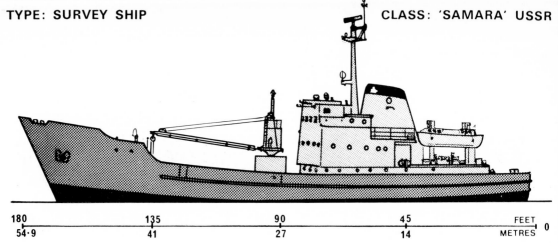

| 180 | 135 | 90 | 45 | FEET |
| 54·9 | 41 | 27 | 14 | 0 METRES |

Displacement, tons: 800 standard, 1 000 full load
Dimensions, metres: 54·9 × 9·9 × 3·5 (180 × 33 × 12 ft)
Main machinery: Diesels
Speed, knots: 16
Building dates: 1962 onwards

NOTES: In service in: USSR (18). A standard class of Soviet survey ship.

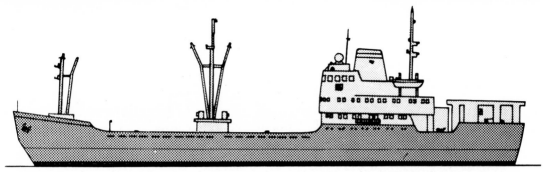

| 401 | 300 | 200 | 100 | FEET | 0 |
| 122 | 91 | 61 | 30 | METRES | |

Measurement, tons: 2 215 net, 6 450 deadweight,
  4 896 gross
Dimensions, metres: 122 × 16·7 × 4·2 (401 × 54·8
  × 14·5 ft)
Main machinery: B & W 9-cyl diesels
Speed, knots: 15

NOTES: In service in: USSR(9). All ex-timber ships now fitted for helicopter operations and part of the Soviet research fleet.

TYPE: SURVEY SHIP   **CLASS: 'NIKOLAI ZUBOV' USSR**

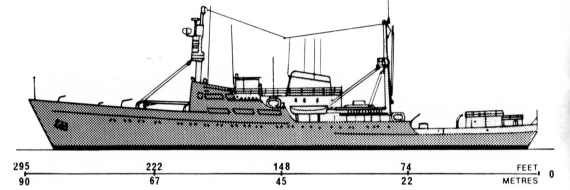

295	222	148	74	FEET
90	67	45	22	METRES 0

Displacement, tons: 2 674 standard, 3 021 full load
Dimensions, metres: 90 × 13 × 4·5 (295 × 43 × 15 ft)
Main machinery: 2 diesels

Speed, knots: 16·7
Complement: 108-120
Building dates: 1964 onwards

NOTES: In service in: USSR (12). Another well-known class of Soviet research ship.

TYPE: HOVERCRAFT   CLASS: 'WINCHESTER' (SR.N6) IRAN
UK

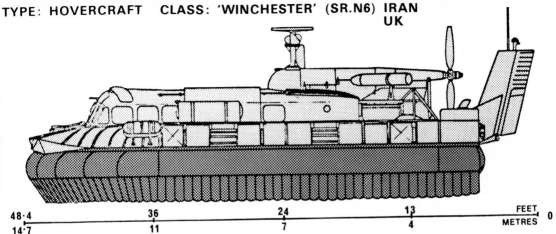

48·4	36	24	13	FEET	0
14·7	11	7	4	METRES	

Displacement, tons: 10 normal gross weight (basic weight 14 200 lb, disposable load 8 200 lb)
Dimensions, metres: 14·7 × 7·7 × 4·8 (height) (48·4 × 25·3 × 15·9 ft (height))

Main machinery: 1 Gnome Model 1 050 gas turbine; 1 Peters diesel as auxiliary power unit
Speed, knots: 58 max

NOTES: In service in: Iran (8), UK (1).   Included to illustrate a productive field of naval design.

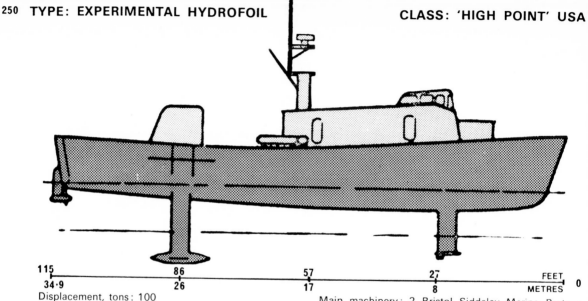

115	86	57	27	FEET
34·9	26	17	8	METRES 0

Displacement, tons: 100
Dimensions, metres: 34·9 × 9·4; draught 1·8 to 5·1
 (115 × 31 × 6/17 ft)
Guns: 2—·50 cal MG (twin)
A/S weapons: 4—21 in torpedo launchers (2 twin),
 DCT

Main machinery: 2 Bristol Siddeley Marine Proteus
 gas turbines, 6 200 shp; 2 shafts
Speed, knots: 48 max
Complement: 13
Building dates: 1961-63

NOTES: In service in: USA (1). Included to illustrate a development in which great advances may be made. In Canada, China, Italy and the USSR much has been done, as well as with the four hydrofoils now with the USN. This type is also being discussed in the UK.

GLOSSARY

ENGLISH	FRANÇAIS
Battleship	Bâtiment de ligne
Aircraft carrier	Porte-avions (PA)
Aircraft carrier (helicopter)	Porte-hélicoptères (PH)
Patrol submarine (SS)	Sous-marin d'attaque (SM)
Fleet submarine (SSN)	Sous-marin nucléaire d'attaque (SNA)
Ballistic missile submarine (SSBN)	Sous-marin lance-missiles balistiques
Cruise missile submarine (SSGN)	Sous-marin lance-missiles aérodynamiques
Cruiser	Croiseur (Cr)
Missile cruiser (CG)	Croiseur lance-engins (CLE)
Cruiser (helicopter)	Croiseur porte-helicopteres
Assault ship	Transport chaland de débarquement (TCD)
LST	Bâtiment de débarquement (BDC)
LCT	Engin de débarquement (EDIC)
Destroyer	Contre-torpilleur (CT)
Missile destroyer (DLG)	Frégate lance-engins (FLE)
Frigate	Frégate
Corvette	Corvette
Missile boat	Vedette lance-engins
Torpedo boat	Vedette lance-torpilles
Patrol craft	Patrouilleur
Minelayer	Mouilleur de mines
Fleet minesweeper	Dragueur océanique
Coastal minesweeper	Dragueur côtier
Support ship	Bâtiment de soutien logistique (BSL)
Survey ship	Bâtiment hydrographe
Research ship	Bâtiment de recherche scientifique
Hydrofoil	Hydroptère
Hovercraft	Hydroglisseur

ENGLISH	FRANÇAIS
Displacement	Déplacement
Standard	Standard
Full	En pleine charge
Dimensions	Dimensions
Feet	Pieds
Metres	Mètres
Aircraft	Avion
Missiles	Engins
Guns	Canons
Torpedo tubes	Tubes lance-torpilles
Mines	Mines
Main machinery	Appareil moteur
Speed, knots	Vitesse, noeuds
Complement	Equipage
Range	Rayon d'action
Building dates	Dates de construction
Special features	Caractéristiques
Notes	Observations
Type	Type
Class	Classe
Country	Nation

ENGLISH	DEUTSCH	ENGLISH	DEUTSCH
Battleship	Schlachtschiff	Displacement	(Wasser) Verdrängung
Aircraft carrier	Flugzeugträger	Standard	Standard
Aircraft carrier (helicopter)	Hubschrauberträger	Full	Max.
Patrol submarine (SS)	U-Boot	Dimensions	Abmessungen
Fleet submarine (SSN)	Atom-U-Boot	Feet	Fussen
Ballistic missile submarine (SSBN)	Lenkwaffen-U-Boot (SSBN)	Metres	Meteren
Cruise missile submarine (SSGN)	Lenkwaffen-U-Boot (SSGN)	Aircraft	Flugzeug
Cruiser	Kreuzer	Missiles	Raketen
Missile cruiser (CG)	Lenkwaffen Kreuzer	Guns	Geschützen
Cruiser (helicopter)	Hubschrauber Kreuzer	Torpedo tubes	Torpedorohren
Assault ship	Landungsführungsschiff	Mines	Minen
LST	Landungsschiff	Main machinery	Hauptantrieb
LCT	Landungsboot	Speed, knots	Geschwindigkeit, Knoten
Destroyer	Zerstörer	Complement	Besatzung
Missile destroyer (DLG)	Lenkwaffenzerstörer	Range	Aktionsradius
Frigate	Fregatte	Building dates	Fertigstellung
Corvette	Korvette	Special features	Besonderheiten
Missile boat	Lenkwaffenboot (FK-S-Boot)	Notes	Sonstige Angaben
		Type	Schiffstyp
Torpedo boat	Schnellboot	Class	Klasse
Patrol craft	Wachboot	Country	Nation
Minelayer	Minenleger		
Fleet minesweeper	Minensucher		
Coastal minesweeper	Küstenminensuchboot		
Support ship	Trossschiff		
Survey ship	Vermessungsschiff		
Research ship	Erprobungsschiff		
Hydrofoil	Tragflächenboot		
Hovercraft	Luftkissenfahrzeug		

ENGLISH	ITALIANO	ENGLISH	ITALIANO
Battleship	Nave da battaglia	Displacement	Dislocamento
Aircraft carrier	Portaerei	Standard	Stendardo
Aircraft carrier (helicopter)	Portaelicotteri	Full	Stazza
Patrol submarine (SS)	Sommergibile	Dimensions	Dimensioni
Fleet submarine (SSN)	Sottomarino d'attacco	Feet	Piede
Ballistic missile submarine (SSBN)	Sottomarino lanciamissli balistici	Metres	Metri
Cruise missile submarine (SSGN)	Sottomarino lanciamissili	Aircraft	Aerei
		Missiles	Missili
Cruiser	Incrociatore	Guns	Cannoni
Missile cruiser (CG)	Incrociatore lanciamissili	Torpedo tubes	Tubi lanciasiluri
Cruiser (helicopter)	Incrociatore portaelicotteri	Mines	Mine
Assault ship	Nave d'attacco anfibio	Main machinery	Apparato motore principale
LST	Nave da sbarco	Speed, knots	Velociata, nodi
LCT	Unità da sbarco	Complement	Complemento
Destroyer	Cacciatorpediniere	Range	Raggio
Missile destroyer (DLG)	Caccialanciamissili	Building dates	Dati di costruzione
Frigate	Fregata	Special features	Caratteristiche
Corvette	Corvetta	Notes	Note
Missile boat	Vedetta lanciamissili	Type	Tipo
Torpedo boat	Motosilurante	Class	Classe
Patrol craft	Motovedetta	Country	Nazione
Minelayer	Posamine		
Fleet minesweeper	Dragamine		
Coastal minesweeper	Dragamine costiero		
Support ship	Nave appoggio		
Survey ship	Nave idrografica		
Research ship	Nave da ricerca		
Hydrofoil	Aliscafo		
Hovercraft	Hovercraft		

ENGLISH	РУССКИЙ
Battleship	Линкор
Aircraft carrier	Авианосец
Aircraft carrier (helicopter)	Вертолетоносец
Patrol submarine (SS)	Подводная лодка
Fleet submarine (SSN)	Атомная подводная лодка-торпедоносец
Ballistic missile submarine (SSBN)	
Cruise missile submarine (SSGN)	Атомная подводная лодка-ракетоносец
Cruiser	Крейсер
Missile cruiser (CG)	Крейсер с УРС
Cruiser (helicopter)	Крейсер-вертолетоносец
Assault ship	Ударный десантный корабль
LST	Танко-десантный корабль
LCT	Малый танко-десантный корабль
Destroyer	Эсминец
Missile destroyer (DLG)	Эсминец-ракетоносец
Frigate	Сторожевой корабль
Corvette	Корвет
Missile boat	Ракетный катер
Torpedo boat	Торпедный катер
Patrol craft	Сторожевой катер
Minelayer	Минный заградитель
Fleet minesweeper	Эскадренный тральщик
Coastal minesweeper	Базовый тральщик
Support ship	Судно снабжения
Survey ship	Гидрографическое судно
Research ship	Научно-исследовательское судно
Hydrofoil	Катер на подводных крыльях
Hovercraft	Судно на воздушной подушке

ENGLISH	РУССКИЙ
Displacement	Водоизмещение
Standard	Стандартное
Full	Полное
Dimensions	Размерения
Feet	Футы
Metres	Метры
Aircraft	Самолет
Missiles	Ракеты
Guns	Орудие
Torpedo tubes	Торпедные аппараты
Mines	Мины
Main machinery	Главные двигатели
Speed, knots	Скорость хода, узлы
Complement	Экипаж
Range	Дальность плавания
Building dates	Годы постройки
Special features	Специальные особенности
Notes	Примечания
Type	Тип
Class	Класс
Country	Страна

ENGLISH	ESPAÑOL
Battleship	Acorazado
Aircraft carrier	Portaaviones
Aircraft carrier (helicopter)	Portaelicópteros
Patrol submarine (SS)	Submarino de patrulla
Fleet submarine (SSN)	Submarino de flota
Ballistic missile submarine (SSBN)	Submarino lanzaproyectiles balisticos
Cruise missile submarine (SSGN)	Submarino crucero lanzaproyectiles dirigidos
Cruiser	Crucero
Missile cruiser (CG)	Crucero lanzaproyectiles dirigidos
Cruiser (helicopter)	Crucero portaelicópteros
Assault ship	Buque de asalto
LST	Buque de desembarco
LCT	Lancha de desembarco
Destroyer	Destructor
Missile destroyer (DLG)	Destructor lanzaproyectiles dirigidos
Frigate	Fregata
Corvette	Corbeta
Missile boat	Navío lanzaproyectiles dirigidos
Torpedo boat	Torpedero
Patrol craft	Patrullero
Minelayer	Minador
Fleet minesweeper	Dragaminas de flota
Coastal minesweeper	Dragaminas costero
Support ship	Buque de soporte logístico
Survey ship	Buque de hidrografo
Research ship	Buque de investigaciones
Hydrofoil	Hidrodeslizador
Hovercraft	Aerodeslizador

ENGLISH	ESPAÑOL
Displacement	Desplazamiento
Standard	Normal
Full	A plena carga
Dimensions	Dimensiones
Feet	Pies
Metres	Metros
Aircraft	Avión
Missiles	Proyectiles dirigidos
Guns	Cañones
Torpedo tubes	Tubos lanzatorpedos
Mines	Minas
Main machinery	Maquinaria principal
Speed, knots	Velocidad, nudos
Complement	Dotación
Range	Radio de acción
Building dates	Fechas de construcción
Special features	Características especiales
Notes	Notas
Type	Tipo
Class	Clase
Country	País

INDEXES

GENERAL INDEX

Abbreviations in ( ) following the name of the ship indicate the country of ownership.

INDEX BY CLASSES

Abbreviations in ( ) following the name of the class indicate the country of ownership. The abbreviations used are the same as in the General Index.